EXPERT SYSTEMS
Programming in Turbo C®

This book is dedicated to Mayor John Marlow,
Councilmen Michael Kitts, Walter Duncan,
Ed Pomeroy, and Councilwoman Sally Miller
who have proven to be interesting colleagues
and valued friends.

EXPERT SYSTEMS
Programming in Turbo C®

Frederick Holtz

Published by **Windcrest Books**
FIRST EDITION/FIRST PRINTING

© 1989 by **Windcrest Books**. Reproduction or publication of the content in any manner, without express permission of the publisher, is prohibited. The publisher takes no responsibility for the use of any of the materials or methods described in this book, or for the products thereof.

Library of Congress Cataloging-in-Publication Data
Holtz, Frederick.
    Expert systems programming in turbo C / by Frederick Holtz.
      p. cm.
    Includes index.
    ISBN 0-8306-2990-4 (pbk.)
    1. Expert systems (Computer science) 2. C (Computer program language) 3. Turbo C (Computer program) I. Title.
QA76.76.E95H67 1989
006.3'3—dc19   88-36526
                                                                  CIP

TAB BOOKS Inc. offers software for sale. For information and a catalog, please contact TAB Software Department, Blue Ridge Summit, PA 17294-0850.

Questions regarding the content of this book should be addressed to:
Windcrest Books
Division of TAB BOOKS Inc.
Blue Ridge Summit, PA 17294-0850

Acquisitions Editor: Ron Powers
Technical Editor David M. Harter
Production: Katherine Brown
Book Design: Jaclyn B. Saunders

Contents

	Introduction	vii
1	***C and Artificial Intelligence***	1
	C Language Applications 7	
	C Language and Artificial Intelligence 8	
	Summary	
2	***Turbo C***	11
	System Requirements 14	
	Writing and Running a First Program 16	
	File 18	
	Edit 19	
	Run 20	
	Compile 20	
	Project 21	
	Options 21	
	Debug 23	
	Using Turbo C 24	
	Comparing Turbo C 25	
	Compiler Memory Models 26	
	Leaving the Integrated Environment 28	
	TCC 29	
	Optimization 30	
	Summary 31	
3	***Truth, Chance and Statistics***	33
	The Laws of Chance 35	
	C Language Probability Functions 48	
	Summary 60	
4	***Game Playing***	61
	Math and Music 63	
	Simple Emulation of Human Thought 69	
	Summary 95	
5	***Data Management for AI Systems***	79
	Virtual File Keeping Functions 80	
	Summary 95	

6 Expert Systems   **97**

    The Expert Plumber   99
    "Is It a Mammal?"   102
    Toward a Generic Expert   110
    Learning by Trial and Error   121
    Saving the Information   127
    Pattern Recognition   129
    Expert Guessing   143
    An Expert System   159
    Summary   166

A Listings for Chapter 3   **167**

B Listings for Chapter 4   **173**

C Listings for Chapter 5   **179**

D Listings for Chapter 6   **185**

Index   **205**

Introduction

Expert systems, artificial intelligence, machines that think—these ideas were the output of science fiction only a few years ago. Today, the concepts of artificial intelligence, as used in expert systems, encompass a significant corner of computer research, and this field of study is being put to practical use more and more each day.

Artificial intelligence is no longer only a dream of futurist authors. The vestiges of machine intelligence are now available for practical applications. Both computers and software are delving deeper into, and going farther toward, true machine intelligence.

In this century, machines will mimic human thinking in certain areas to such a degree that an average human might not know he is talking with a machine. No, this level of artificial intelligence has not, presently, been reached—but every day there are teams of scientists, programmers, psychologists, and others who are reaching out for machine intelligence.

Even though artificial intelligence is still thought of as being in its infancy, many years of progress have been made, and the infant is possibly approaching teenager status. Initially, many efforts aimed at artificial intelligence dealt with how to make a machine think like a human being. In more recent years, however, AI explorers have generally come to the conclusion that if it seems to think like a human being, appears to do so, or offers the information that a human being might be called upon to deliver, then such a program is indeed soundly within the realm of artificial intelligence.

The C language has not been especially associated with expert systems and artificial intelligence. Other languages such as LISP, PROLOG, etc., are more commonly thought of as languages that address AI in a standardly appropriate manner. The C language, however, has become almost a universal language—especially where microcomputers are involved. It is therefore understandable that C is being heavily used today in artificial intelligence endeavors.

This book is aimed at the moderate level C language user who has a yen to explore the beginning concepts of artificial intelligence in expert systems. The text guides you from simple game playing to the establishment of fast-access data bases and, finally, into the realm of the expert system. As opposed to approaching the science of artificial intelligence from a purely theoretical point of view, this text concentrates on the practical aspects. Therefore, you will find a large number of C programs that are, for the most part, completely functioning entities which perform practical or instructional functions. It is one thing to discuss the theoretical operations of an expert system and another to show a working example. This book concentrates on the latter teaching concept.

I have tried to present programs that offer some common points of reference in the general uses of the C programming language. Additionally, some new methods are also presented in C language source code constructs that may look foreign at first sight. However, the text explanation that accompanies each program should clear things up. Many programs are largely explained on a line-by-line basis. The more adept C programmer may wish to skip over such detailed explanations. The moderate level user, however, should find them extremely helpful in understanding not only expert systems programming, but also newer aspects of C programming.

I hope that the materials contained in the following chapters will allow you to become more actively involved in the highly interesting pursuit of export systems and artificial intelligence, while adding to your knowledge of the C programming language and its many uses.

1

C and Artificial Intelligence

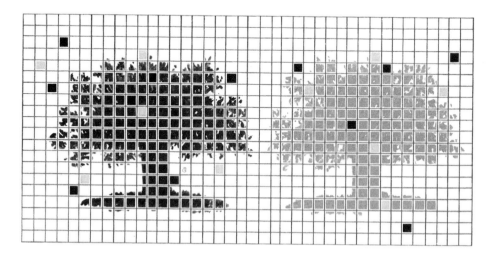

The C language is a moderate level language that was developed over a decade ago by an avant garde team of programmers at Bell Laboratories in New Jersey. C was not even an official Bell Labs project at the beginning but a pet pastime of a group of highly competitive young programmers. It seems that each tried to outdo the other by adding something new and different to the language. The name, C, was chosen because the language took a large part of its characteristics from a portion of another language known as BCPL, with C being the second letter of the larger language.

Regardless of the facts that surround the development of this language, C saw little general usage for about ten years. Those that did program in C were made up almost entirely of the upper crust of the professional programming community. C, then, was the tool of the system programmer. Just prior to the middle of this decade, C boomed forth as one of the most desirable languages yet available for general-purpose programming.

The popularity of C can be attributed to many reasons, most of them arguable. However, the portability of C is a main factor.

Assembly language programs still provide the fastest execution speeds when compared with all other practical methods of programming, but C language offers very fast execution times in comparison. Of course, execution speed is usually a high priority attribute. However, programs written in Assembler are not generally portable from computer to computer. Therefore, a program written in Assembler for one type of microprocessor must be rewritten entirely if it is to run on a machine that uses a different microprocessor. C language offers far greater portability than does Assembler, and without a vast reduction in execution speed as would be the case with most other high-level languages.

C is often called a high-level language—and, indeed, it does possess many of the characteristics of one. However, it also possesses the characteristics of a low-level language. The authors of C have referred to it as a "relatively low-level language" or a moderate level language. What does all this mean?

To begin, here is a comparison of various languages. BASIC is a high-level language, and Assembler may be thought of as a low-level language. C lies somewhere in between. A high-level language like BASIC offers a lot of built-in conveniences. Many of its statements and functions do amazingly complex things like return substrings, clear the screen, position the cursor based upon a pair of coordinates, etc.

On the other hand, Assembler offers just the primitive building blocks that may allow you to, eventually, arrive at the operations you want but on a byte-by-byte construction basis.

I like to explain programming with languages of various levels in terms of building a house. A program built from a high-level language like BASIC is like a house built from prefabricated components. For instance, the staircase is delivered to the builder already complete and ready for installation. The roof is already assembled into one or two pieces; door frames are constructed ahead of time and need only be positioned, nailed into place, and painted; walls are installed in large sections.

On the other hand, the program written in a low-level language like Assembler is like the house that is built on a brick-by-brick basis. The roof must be constructed from individual pieces of lumber, covered with plywood sections, and finished a shingle at a time. Door frames are built from unfinished pieces of lumber that must be measured and cut to size, nailed together, erected, etc.

The high-level house is more easily constructed, because it is assembled from prefabricated sections. It goes together faster and with far less effort. However, the high-level house also greatly restricts the addition of any custom features. If wall panels designate a room that is 14 feet by 20 feet, then that's what you're stuck with. If you want to enlarge or shrink the room by a foot or so, you're out of luck. The panels are designed for the room to be one size and that is the size it must be.

The low-level house is more difficult to build, because little has been done for you ahead of time. Everything must be constructed from individual bricks and boards. However, this house offers the ultimate in customizing. Because the builder constructs the wall panels on-site, the dimensions of any room may be determined just prior to their construction.

When talking computer programming, you can say that a program written in a high-level language goes together quite rapidly, providing that you stick to the operations provided by that language's functions, statements, variables, and other elements that make up the language as a whole. You are using programming components that have been assembled for you from primitives.

However, you are restricted when trying to write a custom feature. For instance, assume that you want (heaven only knows why) a function in BASIC that will return a substring that is composed of the left two characters in the target string followed by the right two characters in the target string. With an argument of the string, "COMPUTER", this function, let's call it RILEF$, would return the substring, "COER". How would you go about constructing such a function?

First off, you really can't construct a new function in standard, Microsoft BASIC, because this is not permitted directly. However, you can write it as a subroutine. The subroutine code might appear as:

```
400  A$=LEFT$(R$,2)
410  B$=RIGHT$(R$,2)
420  C$=A$+B$
430  RETURN
```

This assumes that the target string is contained in R$. The RILEF$ substring will be contained in C$ when the subroutine is exited. This could be shortened considerably, although with more confusion, via the following subroutine:

```
400 C$=LEFT$(R$,2)+RIGHT$(R$,2):RETURN
```

Either way, the left two and right two characters in R$ are returned to C$ as a substring.

Now, this may not seem like such a difficult construction, especially to readers who may still program a lot in BASIC. However, this is quite inefficient from a programming standpoint, although this may be the only good way to accomplish what you want in BASIC.

To program this operation, it is necessary to use what is available to us and LEFT$ and RIGHT$ seem the most appropriate (or the least objectionable) functions to use as "primitives" to construct RILEF$. However, these two standard BASIC functions are not really primitives. They are complex functions that are built from primitives, and they require a certain amount of execution time to carry out their operations.

Assuming that they each take the same amount of time to extract a substring, both functions operating together will require twice the execution time. Therefore, this subroutine is not as efficient from an execution speed standpoint as it could be, because we are using two functions in a combination. Neither does exactly what we are looking for, but in combination we can use their operations for our purposes.

This is a good example of a restriction run into when programming in a high-level language. Now, if execution speed is of little or no importance (and it almost always is), then there is little or no problem. However, if it is important, then you are stuck with a less-than-efficient operation.

On the other hand, the prospect of programming an equivalent of RILEF$ in Assembler would present few problems from an efficiency standpoint. First of all, the equivalents of LEFT$ and RIGHT$ would not even exist. Therefore, RILEF$ would be built from scratch, using primitives. The final product of this operation would be a construct that would return the left two and right two characters in a target string with the highest level of efficiency.

Of course, it will take longer to write such a routine in Assembler, because we are dealing with primitives. The increase in program efficiency over that produced by the high-level language example is obtained at the expense of programmer time.

Here is where a moderate level or relatively low-level language can provide a big payoff. Such a language typically contains a fair number of functions and statements that provide conveniences associated with high-level languages but also provide the basic building blocks in the form of primitives or near-primitives. C is such a language, and this is the key to its great versatility.

The C function in FIG. 1-1 will return a substring equal to the left-most two and right-most two characters in its target string. This is a very simple function that assumes the target string represented by char *r contains at least 4 characters in addition to the terminating NULL. If additional safety features are to be added, this would require a few more lines of code. Nevertheless, the point is made.

This function is easily constructed and operates with a high degree of efficiency. It does this because it is designed to do one thing and one thing only. It returns the left-most two and right-most two characters in a

Fig. 1-1. This function returns the left- and right-most two characters.

```
char *rilef(r)
char *r;
{
        char a[5];
        int x = strlen(r) - 2;

        a[0] = *r;
        a[1] = *(r + 1);
        a[2] = *(r + x);
        a[3] = *(r + x + 1);
        a[4] = '\0';

        return(a);

}
```

Fig. 1-2. This function is the equivalent of BASIC's LEFT$.

```
char *left(r, x)
char *r;
int x;
{
        int y;
        char a[20]
        for (y = 0; y < x; ++y)
                a[y] = *r++;

        a[y] = '\0';

        return(a);

}
```

string. It is not constructed from other functions, although it does use the strlen( ) function as a convenience. Even here, strlen( ) is probably the most efficient way to determine the length of a string in C. You could try to improve on this function (you have that capability in C, but not in BASIC), but you probably couldn't improve its execution efficiency.

But what about LEFT$ and RIGHT$ equivalents in C? Again, this is a moderate level language. Some complex functions are provided for you, but you have to build most on your own. The function in FIG. 1-2 is the C equivalent of BASIC's LEFT$. This simple function returns the left-most x characters in r. Again, certain safety features have been omitted for the sake of simplicity. This function assumes that there are at least x characters in the target string r. Again, this is a very efficient function, because it is simple and intended to do one thing: return the left-most character in the target string specified. It is a completely different function from the one previously presented, although they both return substrings.

To go a step farther, the function in FIG. 1-3 mimics the operation of RIGHT$ in BASIC. Again, we have a completely different function from the previous two. Like its cousins, right( ) operates very efficiently, because it is designed for one purpose.

Now having constructed C equivalents of LEFT$ and RIGHT$, we could fall back on the principle used in BASIC and write another rilef( ) function as shown in FIG. 1-4. This function will do the same as the previous rilef( ), but the execution speed efficiency will be very, very poor in comparison. Why? Because the code that causes the proper value to be returned is so much longer and, thus, more complex. There are more lines of code to execute, so the execution takes longer. The first rilef( ) example was only 8 lines of code within its function body. The above example contains many

Fig. 1-3. This function mimics the operation of RIGHT$ in BASIC.

```
char *right(r, x)
char r[];
int x;
{
        char a[20];
        int y, z;

        y = strlen(r) - x;
        z = 0;

        while (a[z] = r[y + z++])
            ;

        return(a);

}
```

Fig. 1-4. This is a much slower version of rilef ( )

```
char *rilef(r)
char r[];
{
        char c[100];

        strcpy(c, left(r, 2));
        strcat(c, right(r, 2));

        return(c)
}
```

times this amount, because we have to also add in the code lines for right( ), left( ), strcpy( ), and strcat( ). Even though the latter two functions are part of the standard C library, they do contain lines of code that have to be executed. The more functions we use to build another function, the longer the execution time.

It is hoped that this discussion and the examples provided have adequately demonstrated the difference in a high-, moderate, and low-level computer language. In summary, the high-level language offers the epitome in programming ease through prewritten complex statements and functions. The low-level language offers the ultimate in versatility through primitives that are used to build statements and functions. Finally, the moderate level language offers both high- and low-level attributes for a compromise between absolute ease of programming and absolute versatility.

C LANGUAGE APPLICATIONS

It has only been within the latter half of the 1980s that C language has become very popular with major software developers on an almost universal basis. Previous to this, most of the microcomputer software that was marketed to hundreds of thousands of users was written in Assembler. When the portable nature of C was realized, along with its excellent execution speed, these same software companies began rewriting many of their most popular programs in C and most new software projects were begun in this language.

While someone learning C may not agree, this language is quite small and simple. It possesses a small number of functions, an even smaller number of statements, and offers a straightforward control flow. However, its syntax is quite odd, especially to those making the transition from BASIC language. Again, C is a small language and it can be learned quite quickly once the unusual aspects of its syntax are mastered.

Now, while C language is quite fast, or more accurately, the machine code that is compiled from the source code of a program written in C is quite fast, it does not match the speeds attainable with Assembler. In many applications, this is unimportant. In others it is. However, most speed disadvantages are overcome by calling Assembler routines from C language. Such routines are inserted in a C program at a point where the normal C constructs become too slow in the execution chain. The same thing is done in BASIC when a machine language routine is needed (via the CALL statement in many instances).

Initially, a complex program may be written entirely in C. After it is "up and running," it is pushed through many, many tests, some of which outline areas where execution speed is significantly slowed. These (usually) small portions of the program are then rewritten in Assembler for a significant speed increase. Certainly, the Assembler portion of the overall program will not be portable and will have to be rewritten if the program is to be run on another microprocessor, but only this portion need be altered. The bulk of the program is still in C language, and should be quickly brought up on the new microprocessor.

This portability, then, is one of the most desirable attributes of C language when coupled with the compact code and fast execution speed of programs compiled from this language.

C LANGUAGE AND ARTIFICIAL INTELLIGENCE

C language is often not the first choice of programmers who are working exclusively in the area of artificial intelligence. Traditionally, list- and object-oriented languages like LISP and PROLOG are most associated with AI applications. However, we must return to the touted portability and speed of C language discussed earlier. Today, AI programs are not the proud accomplishments of some scientist, tucked away on a university campus. Rather, such programs are highly marketable and often can and do bring outrageously high prices. (Have you priced a broad-range expert system lately?)

When AI-based programs became a commercial entity, C language automatically entered the picture. Today, there are many different types of computers in common usage in the business and general commercial marketplace. Those users who concentrate mainly within the microcomputer environment may only be concerned with IBM PC compatibility or Macintosh/Apple II compatibility. However, this same group may lose sight of the large and varied host of minicomputers that abound. Not too many years ago, the mini and the micro were in two different worlds and never the twain shall meet. Also, the mini and micro marketplaces were two, completely different fields as far as software vendors were concerned. Neither of these alienations is the case today.

Today's software vendors must look at both markets. More and more, software is being written in a manner that allows the companies that spend their millions of dollars of software development money to sell to several different markets. This pinpoints the minicomputer and the microcomputer, both of which may be used concurrently in the same environment. To serve both of these markets, it is becoming mandatory for software to be compatible with both classes of machines. This is in addition to software compatibility across the myriad configurations within the same class.

Put simply, if you want to market software in the best way possible, your program better have the capability of running on just about every type of popular computer out there. C language goes a long way toward meeting this need. Again, an entire program may not be written in C. However, as much of it as is practical is written in this language with assembly language code being used in the speed-critical and some non-portable code segment areas.

This means that the finished program can be quickly brought up on another type of system by using most of the current C language source code and simply rewriting those portions of the program in the assembler for this new machine. This allows an established program to be brought up on a brand new system in days or weeks instead of months or many months.

The hardest thing about writing artificial intelligence programs is grasping the concept of AI programming in general. Once the concept has been learned, many languages will suffice. Some are better than others from a pure AI programming standpoint. However, when other considerations become important, then the choice of the language may become an all encompassing proposition. This is somewhat the case with C language and artificial intelligence.

C language offers the portability and the speed which are not found in the languages more commonly associated with AI. The manipulation of lists may be a little more readily performed with these other languages, but the extra effort involved in using C is worthwhile when the execution speed and marketing advantages are taken into account.

SUMMARY

C language was not designed specifically for artificial intelligence programming, as is the case with LISP and PROLOG. Rather, C is a general purpose language that can be readily adapted to many different programming applications—including AI. C offers the advantage of high execution speed, excellent portability and a high level of expression. These last advantages make C one of the most appropriate languages for commercial development of artificial intelligence software.

The AI market realizes the advantages of C language. Many companies that market limited AI products based on the other languages are now rewriting their AI programs in C for portability to other systems. More and more, AI-based companies are seeking out knowledgeable C language programmers and writing all current programs entirely in C.

2
Turbo C

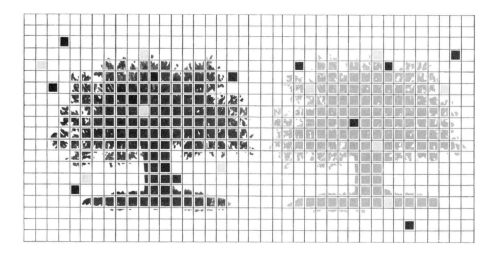

The C program examples throughout this book were written and compiled using the Borland Turbo C compiler version 1.5. This compiler was chosen, because of its popularity. Though one of the newest C compilers on the market, Turbo C became an instant success due to its exceptionally fast compile and execution times, and to its low price (less than $100 retail). Without a doubt, Turbo C is a professional software development environment that incorporates many user-friendly features that benefit the novice programmer as well as the pro.

Additionally, Turbo C adheres closely to the new ANSI standard developed for the C programming language. It offers function prototyping that can simplify certain program operations, making this an ideal environment for the person who is making the switch from BASIC to C. The following discussions overview the Turbo C package for those readers who do not currently have a C language environment and for those who are thinking about switching to this new, fast, and inexpensive C programming language. The speed of compilation along with the fast execution speed make Turbo C an ideal environment for artificial intelligence programming where applications tend to be quite long and speed intensive.

Borland's Turbo C consists of four distribution disks and two manuals. The Turbo C user's manual contains approximately 300 pages, while the Turbo C reference manual is nearly 400 pages in length. The user's manual provides an excellent step-by-step introduction to setting up and using Turbo C. New users of C language will appreciate this type of introduction as will more experienced users who are accustomed to the traditional "hashing out" procedure often required when starting out with new C environments.

This manual also provides some good background information about programming in C language in general. While certainly not a tutorial on the entire C language, this section may prove to be a convenient reference source for beginners.

The manual does leave a bit to be desired when explaining some of the more elaborate features of Turbo C. Beginners will probably get bogged down by some of the language. However, many of these features won't be used immediately by these beginners. By the time their C experience has reached the level where advanced features can be used, their grasp of C "slanguage[sic]" should enable them to pick up on most of the industry buzz words.

One point to remember is that Turbo C is not just a basic C programming environment. It offers an interactive users menu that grizzled, dyed-in-the-wool oldtimers love to hate. Such a menu, however, is an ideal learning environment for newcomers to C. Turbo C satisfies both parties. The user of the menu is optional. Alternate compiling methods which follow the more traditional "command line" approach should make those programmers who shun menus quite happy.

From my standpoint, I almost always use the menu. Oh, I have written four or five batch files to take care of some specialized needs, but the menu suffices 95 percent of the time. Sometimes, I think there is a tendency on the part of long time C programmers to purposely stop the march of progress in the area of "easier-to-use". This might be equated with the homeowner who still prefers to cut his lawn with a scythe while shunning the power lawn mower. Such people are said to be "colorful," "eccentric" (if they also have money), or "crazy" (if they don't).

In C programming, good arguments can be made for interactive menus and just as good arguments can be made against them. If the truth be known, there are times when the menu is a big help and others where it gets in the way. Turbo C programmers may use either or both methods of interfacing with this C compiler.

In a nutshell, Turbo C contains a complete C compiler. This is not a subset of the original language. Rather it is a superset, containing all the original C language offered and a lot more.

Most of the functions and statements available to the programmer in Turbo C will be familiar to users of Lattice C, Microsoft C and Mark Williams C. Microsoft C (Version 4.0) is probably the closest match to Turbo C with regard to each environments list of functions and general usage. This is a qualified statement, because all of the excellent compilers mentioned are closely aligned, and it is usually a simple matter to modify a program written for one to enable it to be compiled under any one of the others. This points to the fact that, from a programming standpoint, all of these compilers are very similar. Therefore, it may be most appropriate to state that Turbo C fits right in with all of these (the former Big Three) from the programmers point of view. However, the programmers who designed Turbo C obviously must have taken a close, hard look at the most popular C compilers for MS-DOS machines and decided to take what was best from each one. Turbo C functions seem to be composite of the functions in these three other compilers.

For instance, Microsoft C offers programmable far pointers for mixed memory model operations and several functions that can move data anywhere in RAM. On the other hand, it does not offer a peek or poke function, as such. Certainly, you can easily peek and poke from the small model compiler using far pointers, movedata( ), or other functions. The lattice C compiler, on the other hand, offers discrete peek( ) and poke( ) functions to be used within the small memory models. So does Turbo C. Of course, Turbo C conforms closely to the new ANSI standard for the C programming language. All compiler models are drifting in this direction, some more so than others.

Turbo C also offers some new functions that address text handling, memory management, interface with DOS files, etc. This is a new and exciting C programming environment that really offers no unpleasant surprises for those of us who have used other compilers. Several pleasant surprises are in store for the experienced user, and this chapter will highlight some of them.

If you are a newcomer to C who has chosen (or is considering) the Turbo C Compiler, then your choice is a wise one. I am unaware of any other full featured C programming environment that offers the user friendliness of Turbo C. In my opinion, the most friendly C programming environment for BASIC programmers today is the RUN/C Interpreter, because this offers several built-in BASIC-like functions like cls( ), locate( ), and others not found in most C packages. However, this interpreter cannot match the speed of a compiler, and a compiler will eventually be necessary for serious program development.

Of special importance, the Turbo C package compiles programs very rapidly. This is a decided plus, in that your programs can be up and running in seconds, instead of minutes with several other good compilers. This also means that programs which contain errors will be detected faster during the rapid compile and linking stages offered by Turbo C.

The advantage of an interpreter lies in its ability to immediately begin running source code without going through a compiling stage. The disadvantage is the slow execution speed, an inherent by-product.

Turbo C is as fast as any of the popular compilers on the market. In fact, it is faster. And, it compiles faster too. And, while you can't run a source program immediately, you can run it within 25 to 45 seconds if the program is small. This is a good trade-off: Fast compile times combined with extremely fast execution. This allows the Turbo C programming package to be a good training environment for newcomers, and is perfectly adequate to take care of professional programming needs as these students become proficient in C.

Turbo C is that rare programming package that grows with the experience level of the programmer. I can think of no reason why those who learn C using Turbo C would need to switch to another compiler after they have gone beyond student status in search of more power. Turbo C is a good investment.

SYSTEM REQUIREMENTS

Turbo C is designed to operate on the IBM PC family of microcomputers, and all close compatibles, running DOS 2.0 and higher. This includes a group of hundreds of microcomputers including the IBM PC, XT, AT, and almost every other machine that is MS-DOS compatible. Each system must be equipped with a minimum of 384K RAM and one 360K disk drive.

Those are the minimum requirements, but let me assure you that using Turbo C with such minimums will be pure hell. The same can likely be said of any other serious development package in C, or any other language.

To really get the full benefit out of Turbo C, your machine should contain at least 512K memory, and 640K is even better. You should have two disk drives at a minimum, although a hard disk is really to be preferred—and is required if you don't want to be pulling your hair out over diskette changes at critical times. The IBM monochrome display, I feel, provides a better programming "window" than does the color display, at least for easily deciphering all of those characters that tend to run together when programming in C for long hours.

The system used as the research model for programs in this book is a standard IBM PC with the 4.77 MHz clock, 640K RAM, IBM Monochrome

Display, Monochrome Display Adapter, Princeton Graphic Systems HX-10 RGB Color Monitor, IBM color card and an 8087 Math Coprocessor.

As far as disks drives are concerned, my system contains two, 360K diskette drives and two 27 megabyte hard disks. This somewhat over-engineered "standard" PC was designed to allow me to test software packages in an environment that would roughly reflect several different "minimum" systems that might be had by the typical user, while not restricting me unnecessarily. The processing speed of this computer is no different from any other IBM PC, and even slower than many clones. I can disregard the hard drives and use one or two diskette drives. I can even configure the machine so that it operates from a single drive and "thinks" it has far less memory than is really on-board. I can even crank in a Turbo board that will triple the processing speed.

Turbo C was run under PC/DOS version 2.1 for most of the research on this book. On a few occasions, I switched to DOS 3.2 in order to test some Turbo C functions that are operable only under this latter system. Most of my commercial software development is done under DOS 2.1 to assure compatibility with the thousands and thousands of PC users who are still operating under these earlier versions. Naturally, programs developed under DOS 2.1 work just fine when run in a higher version.

I have tested Turbo C in all of these configurations and find that a practical minimum, for me, is 512K, a single hard disk, a single floppy disk, and the monochrome display. For other users, these minimums may be conservative or extremely radical. It all depends on what you want to do, how fast you want to do it, and how much inconvenience you can tolerate. For me, using anything but a hard disk with its rapid read/write capabilities is a severe limitation. A turbo processor board is a nice addition, but I find the 4.77 MHz speed of the stock IBM PC to be perfectly comfortable in working with Turbo C, because of its rapid compile times. Of course, turbo boards make the entire package fly.

Owners of IBM PC AT machines and applicable clones should be advised that this is an ideal setting for Turbo C. While I have not tested this programming package on any of the new 386 machines, I am sure these will offer far greater advantages. As a matter of fact, a 10, 12, or even 16 MHz PC AT clone or 386 machine would probably allow Turbo C to act almost like an interpreter for relatively small programs. The compile and linking stages would be handled in just a few seconds and the program could be run almost immediately. Turbo C compiles and links quickly because intermediate files are written to memory, not to the disk drive. This brings about a speed increase which can be described as highly significant.

It should be stressed that speed is essential to any serious excursion into the world of expert systems programming. The system minimums discussed above apply only to exercises within the scope of this text which are aimed at teaching the beginning concepts of artificial intelligence within a C environment. For serious AI applications, these minimums quickly rise to several megabytes of RAM and the fastest microprocessors and clock speeds available.

Programs written in C are inherently faster than programs written in other high level languages. However, this will not overcome the cumbersomely slow (by today's standards) speed of the 4.77 MHz IBM PC, PC XT genre. Again, I am referring to most sophisticated uses of AI. The basic PC was chosen as a standard for this book, because it represents the minimum configuration that any individual within a wide range of readers might have.

If you are equipped with a faster, more modern configuration, then you will immediately benefit from this upgrade. However, if you are using a minimum configuration, you will learn about AI just as rapidly, although you may have to plan to upgrade in order to move into the innermost depths of this pursuit.

WRITING AND RUNNING A FIRST PROGRAM

Turbo C was installed on my hard disk in a directory named \turboc. I established two subdirectories named \turboc\include and \turboc\lib to contain the header files and library files, respectively. All of these could have been amassed into one directory, but this would lend to the confusion. This assortment of directories and sub-directories is pretty much standard when operating in any C environment intended for MS-DOS machines.

Again, \turboc is the master directory from which the interactive menu is accessed. Those persons without a hard disk may think of the three directories I earlier described as three separate floppies named turboc, turbocinclude and turboclib. From this point on, I will make reference only to the directories and subdirectories I initially established on my working model.

In this master directory is a file named TC.EXE which is the Turbo C Integrated Programming Environment, containing the working menu that accesses the compiler, linker, editor, and everything else Turbo C makes use of. Type TC and press Enter. Shortly, a menu will appear on your screen. If you are using a color monitor, then the menu will be multi-colored for best visual clarity. The menu "frame" will be in dark and light blue colors, while the text editor will write in an amber on black window.

It is from this menu that all programs may be written, compiled, linked, and executed. Furthermore, you may also access many other options such as changing the compiler models, debugging, etc. All of these will be overviewed in this chapter. This is a complete interactive environment, allowing you to access nearly all of the possible uses of the Turbo C programming package. There are very few things that can be accomplished with the command line method of compiling programs under Turbo C that cannot also be handled with more convenience from the menu.

There are seven pull-down windows in the Main Menu, plus an on-line HELP utility that is accessed by pressing the F1 function key. The various options are accessed by simultaneously pressing the Alt key plus the key that specifies the first letter of the option you want. For instance, to access the pull-down File menu, you would use the combination: AH–F. This window will be opened, and several options may be chosen by moving the highlight bar via the cursor movement keys.

The Main Menu options are:

File This mini-menu provides options to load, save, pick, create, or write to disk. From this menu you may also list and change directories, temporarily revert to DOS control or exit the Turbo C main menu entirely.

Edit Striking Alt–E invokes the screen editor and allows source programs to be created or edited.

Run The Alt–R combination causes a source program to be compiled, linked, and run in one operation.

Compile The Compile mini-menu provides options to compile and link a source program. Some of these are compile and link, compile only, and link only.

Project The Project menu allows programmers to name all of the files that are associated with a particular program so that this program may be compiled as a single project.

Options The Options menu allows the programmer to select all of the many options offered by the Turbo C package. This includes choosing one of many memory models, compile-time switches, define macros, specify where the header and library files are to be found, etc.

Debug The AH–D key combination allows errors to be tracked.

The following discussions center around the features offered in each of these menus.

FILE

This menu allows the user to select from several choices that involve loading, editing, and saving files. Other choices will allow you to return to the DOS shell (temporarily leave the Turbo C interactive environment), and to display the files in a directory.

The options are chosen by stepping down each selection with the cursor control keys on the numeric keypad. Each selection is highlighted as it is scanned.

Load

The first selection is "Load F3". This can also be immediately accessed by pressing the F3 function key. When this option is chosen, it means that a file is to be loaded into the editor. A window appears on the screen and you may input the name of an existing file to load. If the file does not exist, then this is the name of a new file that may be written and saved. After this choice, Turbo C puts you into the edit window. This full screen editor allows you to begin to immediately write a new program or to edit a program that was just loaded.

Pick

The Pick option in the FILE menu allows you to pick from a list of the last eight files loaded into the editor. If you select one of these, it is loaded into the editor and the cursor is placed at the point where you last left the file. This is very convenient when various programs must be written simultaneously.

New

This option means that the file is a new one and has not been previously named. The file is identified as NONAME.C and will be saved as such unless it is renamed using another option from this menu.

Save

This option saves the current file in the editor to the disk. If the current file is NONAME.C, a window will appear in the editor asking you if you want to change the name. You may do so by simply typing the new name or save it as NONAME.C. If the file has any other name, it is saved immediately under this name, overwriting any other files of the same name.

Write To

This option allows you to write a file contained in the editor as a new name. The new name is given when the window prompt appears.

Directory

As its name implies, this option allows you to get a listing of the contents of any DOS directory. If you press Enter after selecting this option, the current directory appears in its own window.

Change DIR

This option displays the current directory and then prompts for the name of another drive or directory. When this information is provided by the user, the new directory is written to the window.

OS Shell

This option allows you to temporarily exit the Turbo C Interactive Menu and reenter DOS control. You may use the DOS commands as you normally would, but remember that Turbo C stays resident, so you won't have as much memory to work with as before. To return to the Turbo C environment, type exit, and press Enter at the DOS prompt.

Quit

This option allows you to permanently leave the Turbo C interactive menu. If a file is currently contained in the editor that has not been saved to disk, you will be asked if you want to save it before the exit is made. If your response is positive, then the file is saved and the exit is made. If you answer no, then the exit is made immediately, and the program in the editor is lost.

EDIT

The Edit command is invoked from the main menu by the Alt – E key press combination. This puts you into the full screen editor window and allows you to immediately begin writing or editing a loaded program. The editor menu offers no further options, but the screen editor is discussed in more detail later in this chapter.

RUN

The Run command invokes Project-Make, then runs the program in the editor using the arguments given in Options /Args. Project-Make is a program building tool that will be overviewed later in this chapter. Put simply, when you invoke Run, the current program in the editor is compiled, linked and executed. If it has been previously compiled and linked and no changes have been made to the source code, then execution takes place immediately. If you change the source code in any way, invoking Run will bring about the compile/link operations before execution.

COMPILE

The Compile menu offers several options that can produce an object module from the source code in the editor or an EXE file. You can also elect to link a series of object files already in existence with the appropriate library files.

Compile to OBJ

This option is the one to choose if you just wish to compile the source code in the editor. The source code is run through the compiler, the object file is produced, and control is returned to you. The name of the object file will be the same as the source file, only it will have a .OBJ extension.

Make EXE File

This option calls Project-Make. Generally, it takes a program from the editor, compiles it if necessary, and then links it with the appropriate files. The result is an executable version of the source program in the editor.

Link EXE

This option accesses the current object and library files and links them without doing a Make to produce a new EXE file.

Build All

This option unconditionally rebuilds all of the files in a project, regardless of whether or not they are out of date. Unlike Make, which rebuilds only those files that are not current, this option rebuilds all of them.

Primary C File

This option is chosen to specify which source file (.C extension) will be compiled to .OBJ.

PROJECT

The Project menu allows the user to combine multiple source files and object files to create finished programs. This is useful when many source and object files are involved in arriving at a master executable program. This is usually the case when programming most intensive AI operations.

Project Name

This option allows you to select or change the name of a project file. Such a file contains the names of source files to be compiled or linked. This project name will also be the name given to the executable file when it is created.

Break Make On

This option allows you to specify what types of conditions warrant halting the Make operation. You may specify a stop after compiling a file that has warnings, errors, fatal errors, or as a safety routine, before linking.

Clear Project

This option allows you to clear the current project and replace it with another if desired.

OPTIONS

The Options menu is accessed via the Alt-O combination. This is probably the first menu you will access upon entering Turbo C for the first time. This menu contains settings that determine how the Turbo C environment will interact with your system configuration. It also allows you to select a set of "default" criteria, such as computer memory model, code generation, optimization, etc. As a matter of fact, each of the options in this menu offer further options that determine just how Turbo C will compile code, where it will search for library files, whether it is to use register variables, etc.

Compiler

Seven options are available when the Compiler option is accessed. The following list briefly describes each:

Model   This option allows you to select from one of six memory models available in Turbo C. The "Small" memory model is the default. Other models include "Tiny," "Medium," "Compact," "Large," and "Huge".

Defines   This option allows you to specify macro definitions that are always to be a part of any program you compile. Multiple definitions may be input and should be separated by semicolons.

Code Generation   This option offers ten sub-options that cause the compiler to generate either a C language calling sequence, or a Pascal calling sequence for function calls. For all but expert applications, this should be left in the default of C. Another option allows you to specify the instruction set in order to target a specific microprocessor. The default here is 8088/8086, but this can be changed to 80186/80286. Yet another sub-option allows you to determine how floating-point code is generated. You can choose from code that provides floating-point emulation, code that is targeted toward a math coprocessor, and code that uses the coprocessor if available or emulates if it is not.

Optimization   This is an option that you have to experiment with to see the result. This allows you to select the manner in which Turbo C will optimize the code it produces. You can toggle between optimizing for size and optimizing for speed. You can also toggle between using register variables or not. Register optimization can be turned on or off, and jump optimization, when selected, reduces the code size by reorganizing loops and eliminating redundant jumps. More on this later.

Source   The Source option determines how the compiler handles the source code during the start-up phases of compilation. One option allows you to alter the length of identifier names within the range of 1 to 32 characters. Default is 32 characters. You can turn the nested comments option on or off. When it's off, nested comments are not permitted, as per the K&R standard. The last option in this section toggles the ANSI keyword option. When on, the compiler will recognize only ANSI keywords and will treat Turbo C extension keywords as normal identifiers.

Errors This final option determines how the compiler will deal with diagnostic messages. You may specify a halt in compilation after a certain number of errors or warnings have been reported. You can also specify whether or not messages are to be displayed.

Linker

The items in the Linker menu deal with establishing various options for the linker. From this menu, you can select the type of map file to be produced, specify default libraries, disable stack warning messages, and determine whether or not the linker will be case-sensitive.

Environment

The Environment menu allows the Turbo C environment to interact with your system. From this menu, you tell Turbo C where to find the #include files, the library files, and even where to write the output files. You also specify where the Turbo C directory is so that the environment can locate its own help and configuration files. The Auto Save Edit option helps prevent loss of source files by automatically saving a file being edited when you select RUN or temporarily exit to the DOS shell. Several other options allow for custom-tailoring of the Turbo C package to your computer and disk drive configuration.

DEBUG

The final main menu selection is Debug, which offers three options. The first affects the way Turbo C highlights possible problem areas in a source file that has gone through the compilation routine, and resulted in error or warning messages. You can also specify whether these messages are to be retained from edit to edit. You can even turn the message window off completely. A bonus within the Debug window is the listing of the amount of available memory. This will be the memory that is not currently being used by Turbo C to maintain the environment.

This discussion on the main menu has entailed a very very brief overview. Fortunately, highly detailed information is provided in the excellent Turbo C User's Guide. It is hoped that this overview is adequate enough to present a fair description of Turbo C to those readers who have not yet purchased or used this package, but who may be considering it for their C programming environment.

USING TURBO C

The documentation included in the Turbo C User's Manual and the Turbo C Reference Guide is probably worth the price of the entire package. While this book about programming in Turbo C is meant to be instructive, it is certainly belaboring the point to list each and every function and each and every operation that is used with this package. The instructional nature of this book involves making the reader more familiar with Turbo C programming by presenting sample programs (about 200, in fact) along with understandable explanations.

Suffice it to say that if you elect to go with Turbo C, you won't be lacking in documentation on how to interact with this excellent programming system. The following discussions are an overview of my initial reactions to Turbo C as a programming environment, and my continuing experiences working in this realm.

Programmers who are accustomed to C language environments will have little or no problem adapting to Turbo C. Previously, I described how I loaded various Turbo C files into the Turbo C directory and into several subdirectories. At this point, I activated the Turbo C integrated environment by executing the file TC.EXE. This invoked the menu just discussed.

Fortunately, the default settings for this menu require very few changes to begin programming in this environment. The first menu I selected was OPTIONS. Here, I specified that the include directory could be found in \turboc\include. I also instructed the environment as to the location of the library directory, which is \turboc\lib. Everything else was left in the default mode.

The first job is to write a C program. I did this by entering the Alt-E combination at the keyboard. This immediately opened the screen editor, and I quickly hacked out K&R's "hello, world" program. I then entered Alt-C and chose the Make option. In short order, I had a program named NONAME.EXE. I chose to reenter the DOS shell to execute the program. There were no surprises; the program ran as intended.

After several months of using Turbo C, I have developed my own personal habits and routines for writing, compiling and executing code. I normally write the source code and then enter the Make utility via the F9 function key. If I've done my job, this produces an executable file. Rarely do I use the RUN command from the menu. I usually exit temporarily to

DOS, test the program, and then re-enter Turbo C to make changes or add more code.

The editor is not some fantastically new and modern fifth-generation wonder. If you've used the Turbo Pascal or SideKick editor, or even MicroPro's WordStar, then you are already familiar with the Turbo C editor. What can I say? It's an easy editor to use and very easy to learn. It is far superior, in my opinion, to most other editors used for writing programs.

COMPARING TURBO C

As a person who makes his living writing programs in C, teaching C programming, and also writing about programming in C, it is understandable that I would have a significant amount of compilers, libraries, and the general gamut of C programming environments on hand. I do, and I have one or two that I use for the brunt of all my commercial programming endeavors. As of this writing, Turbo C is my programming environment of choice. I have made comparisons of Turbo C with the best compilers the market previously offered. Turbo C seems to come out on top, at least in regard to the properties I feel are important.

As has been stated elsewhere in this book, programs written in Turbo C compile faster, link faster, and run faster than when compiled and linked in these other excellent environments. I'm not specifically naming these others at this time because without a doubt, they too will be improving their products in order to compete with Turbo C and each other: Although a program compiled under Turbo C may run 50 percent faster than one compiled under another environment today, by the time you read these words the slower environment may have been improved to closely match or even exceed what Turbo C can do today. Such are the trends in today's programming environment marketplace.

There is one area, however, that is going to be difficult for the suppliers of these other products to beat. This has to do with the cost of the package itself. Turbo C retails for less than $100, and is being hawked by the mail order houses for less than $70. As mentioned previously, most of the high-level compilers for MS–DOS machines are priced between $350 and $400 retail. Turbo C will probably change this trend toward high-priced C language environments.

As stated earlier, I elected to use a standard 4.77 MHz IBM PC as the hardware model for this text. Compared with other professional compilers, Turbo C compiled and linked my programs at what seemed like lightning speed. For my professional development work, I use a

PC-AT clone with a 12 MHz clock. Turbo C really flies in this environment.

My real surprise came when I noticed the tremendous speed increases I was gaining with Turbo C. Some programs ran as much as 70 percent faster than with a non-optimizing, competitive compiler and 30 percent faster than with another optimizing environment. This made the old IBM PC seem like one of the fast, new machines. When run on the fast, new machines, the results were even more apparent.

Something that impresses me even more is the friendliness of this package. It is an extremely easy environment to become accustomed to and to depend on. After using it for three months, I have no harsh criticisms.

COMPILER MEMORY MODELS

Turbo C, like most modern C compilers, offers several different memory models that may be user-selected. As a matter of fact, Turbo C offers six memory models, which is more than most. Each memory model has its own set of libraries and start-up object files. The memory model you choose to program in is determined by a number of factors, including source code size, object code size, the amount of data storage needed, execution speed, etc. Of the six memory models offered, the default is the "Small" model. This is the one that I have the most experience with, and the one I target for all of my commercial work if at all possible and practical.

Tiny

The Tiny memory model is the smallest of the six offered. It offers a total of 64K for all code, data, and arrays. This model uses only near pointers, and programs compiled under this model can be converted to .COM format, which allows for faster loading and start-up execution of the file. Most small programs will fit the Tiny model if it is not necessary to declare a large number of arrays, or a small number of arrays with very large subscripts.

Small

This memory model is similar to the Tiny model in that near pointers are always used. However, code and data segments are separated and do not overlap. The Tiny model allows a total of 64K for code and data, and the Small model offers 64K for each. Total size is 128K. In the Small memory model, the stack and extra segments start at the same address as the data segment. Borland states that this is a good memory model size for average applications. It can also be used for some of the moderately large applications by using highly efficient programming techniques. I have written several moderately large applications and compiled them under the Small memory model with excellent results.

Because both the Tiny and Small models use near pointers for all operations, these 2-byte entities offer the fastest execution times. Of course, Turbo C also offers the advantage of explicitly programming far pointers from these smaller models, which is also a bonus. In such instances, near and far pointers are intermixed within the same memory model.

Medium

In this model, the data segment is limited to a 64K area, but code can occupy up to 1 MB. Far pointers are used, so execution speed will be slower than with the Tiny and Small models. The Medium model, however, would be used only when the smaller models would not suffice. The Medium model is best for large programs that don't store a lot of data in memory.

Compact

The Small and Medium memory models are fairly standard in most modern C compilers. You don't see Tiny models as often, nor do you see a lot of models that are labeled Compact. In the Turbo C implementation, the Compact model is the reverse of the Medium model. The Compact model uses far pointers for data but uses near pointers for code. The code is limited to a 64K area, while data has a 1 MB range. In the Medium memory model, far pointers are used for code, but not for data. The Compact model might be chosen when program code is small, but it must access a large amount of data.

Large

The Large memory model of the Turbo C compiler sets aside 1 MB for code and 1 MB for data. Only far pointers are used for access, so this model will execute code more slowly than the previous models due to the 4-byte pointer operations involved. The Large memory model should be reserved for very large programs that access an equally large amount of data.

Huge

The Huge memory model is quite similar to the Large model, in that it uses far pointers for both code and data. However, all of the previous models limit the size of all static data to 64K. In the Huge memory model, static data can occupy more than 64K. The total amount is determined by the memory configuration of your computer.

To change memory models, all that is required is to reset the Compiler option in the OPTIONS menu. If all of your library files and object code start-up files are in one directory, making this compiler change will be a one-step operation. It is for this reason that I explained in fair detail how the Turbo C files were installed on my hard disk. If you're operating without a hard disk, you may have a fair amount of disk-swapping operations to perform when switching to a different memory model.

If you are not a highly experienced C programmer, and are just becoming adjusted to Turbo C, it is my recommendation that you start with the Small memory model. This should pose no limitations at all. Most professional programmers who write code for MS-DOS machines try to stay within the roomy confines of models that use the 2-byte pointers.

LEAVING THE INTEGRATED ENVIRONMENT

All of the discussion thus far has centered around the use of Turbo C from the Integrated Development Environment. This is far different than the command line method many C programmers are accustomed to: all commands are issued under DOS via executable files that accept arguments as they are invoked.

Traditionally, professional programmers hate integrated and interactive environments that include everything from handy pull-down menus, to garbage can icons. Some programmers complain that the integrated environment slows them down, while others just don't like adapting to a new, and often better, way of doing things. In any event, Turbo C gives you your choice of environments. If you don't want to use the integrated system with all of its convenient menus and other built-in features, you can go the command line route and invoke the compiler and linker via arguments from DOS.

I did have occasion to leave the Integrated Development Environment and pursue the command line route a few hours after getting into Turbo C. The only real problem with the interactive system is that it does require a fair amount of memory for its own purposes. When you compile programs, no intermediate files are written to disk. They are all written to memory. This is another reason for the fast compile and link times exhibited by Turbo C.

However, using memory to hold these intermediate files consumes more of your precious RAM. My initial test machine was equipped with 512 KB RAM. This was more than sufficient for the compilation and linking of some fairly large applications that ran to several thousand lines of C source code. However, one particularly long and complex program could not be compiled within the integrated environment. Too much memory was consumed by the environment, and the intermediate file that was written to memory.

Turbo C is quite kind to you when you run out of memory in this manner. It simply stops the compiling process and issues an error message stating that it has run out of memory.

Out of necessity, I exited the environment and invoked the command line options to compile and link this program. The procedure took place with no problems at all. Several batch files were later written to allow for similarly large and complex programs to be compiled and linked in the same manner.

TCC

The command line version of Turbo C is contained in the file TCC.EXE. The Turbo Linker program is contained in TLINK.EXE. The command line utilities also include versions of Make, Touch, and similar utilities that can be invoked from the integrated environment.

The available options are quite complete, and allow you to do anything from the command line environment that you can do from the integrated environment. As a matter of fact, you can do a little more from the command line. If you intend to use assembly language routines with your C code (in other words, call assembly language modules from C), you will have to invoke the −B option from the command line version of Turbo C. This can't be done from the integrated menu.

The following shows the contents of a batch file I quickly produced to perform a simple compilation using TCC:

```
tcc −I\turboc\include −ms −c %1
```

This line invokes the −I option to tell the compiler where to find the header files. The −ms option is the default and does not need to be invoked, but is done here for the sake of clarity. This tells the command line version of Turbo C to use the Small memory model compiler. The −c option is a signal to only compile the target program that is represented here as %1.

The next batch file invokes TLINK.EXE, the command line linker:

```
tlink \turboc\lib\c0s + %1,%1,, \turboc\lib\emu| \turboc\lib\cs
```

The arguments to TLINK are the same as the arguments to the MS–DOS linker, LINK.EXE. In this usage, the c0s.OBJ start-up module for the Small memory model is found in the \turboc\lib directory of my hard disk. This module is coupled with the name of the object file output by the compiler. The second %1 tells the linker to give the EXE file the same name as the program object file. The final sequence tells the linker to access EMU.LIB and CS.LIB from the \turboc\lib directory on the default drive.

Compilation and linking are just as rapid when invoked from the command line version of Turbo C. I only use the command line version when it is not possible to compile or link programs because of their size or lack of on-board RAM. Speaking as one who has always operated on a command line basis with C environments, I find that integrated environment to be quicker and more convenient. I have enjoyed making the switch.

OPTIMIZATION

As was pointed out earlier, the user has several optimization choices when using Turbo C. Various types and stages of optimization can be selected via the OPTIONS menu within the integrated environment.

You can toggle between optimizing for size and optimizing for speed. What does this mean? Supposedly, when you optimize for size, the compiler chooses the smallest code sequence possible. When this option is toggled for speed, the compiler chooses the fastest sequence for a given task. At least this is what the manual says.

In fact, a best guess is made in both situations. The guess is sometimes right, but it's often wrong. Sometimes, when you optimize for size, you may get a larger program than if you had optimized for speed. Sometimes, optimizing for speed will result in a slower program than if it had been optimized for size. Just as often, the program will be the same size and will run at the same speed regardless of which optimization method you choose. This is not a criticism of the Turbo C compiler. It just means that a best guess is just that: a guess at what method is best to pursue in arriving at the goal of smaller size or increased speed.

I talked with several of the key people in the Turbo C project at Borland and was told that the best thing to do is to compile programs that may be size- or speed-critical under both options, and then choose the one that yields the best results. I compiled a very large and complex commercial program, initially for size, which resulted in a very impressive execution speed. Then I recompiled it for speed. The code size was about the same, and it ran more slowly by a few percentage points. Obviously, the optimization for size resulted in the best overall performance of the program, and this was the optimization that was finally chosen.

Another optimization selection that you can make involves whether or not register variables are to be used. This is normally ON and, in this state, register variables will automatically be assigned. When it's OFF, the compiler will not use registers for storage of variables. (The source code may still contain the "register" data type, but the compiler simply incorporates them as "auto" variable types.) Again, a best guess is made as to which variables should be register variables, but this option usually results in faster execution times (often marginal) without an increase in code size. With this feature toggled off, even the declaration of variables as type register will have no effect.

Two other optimization options, Register Optimization and Jump Optimization, are normally OFF. The first suppresses redundant load operations by retaining register values, and reusing them where possible. I don't use this option very often because the compiler can't tell when a register has been changed indirectly through the use of a pointer. If this occurs, crashes are sure to follow.

Even though the Jump Optimization is defaulted to OFF, I usually toggle it ON. The programmers at Borland have told me they generally use this optimization as well. This one reduces code size and increases speed—mainly by reorganizing loops and switch statements.

However, don't expect any of these optimizations to make a tremendous amount of difference in either code size or code speed. I certainly urge you to try various combinations, and perhaps a significant performance increase will be had with certain program constructs. These optimizing options are just another aspect of Turbo C that offer the user more control over the programs they write.

SUMMARY

Turbo C is an ideal C language environment for beginning to mid-level C programmers. This is the audience at whom discussions in this text are aimed. However, it is an equally pleasing environment for the professional programmer. For artificial intelligence applications, it offers all that is necessary to move quickly and easily into this programming mode. And, at less than $100 retail, the price is just as pleasing as its performance.

3
Truth, Chance and Statistics

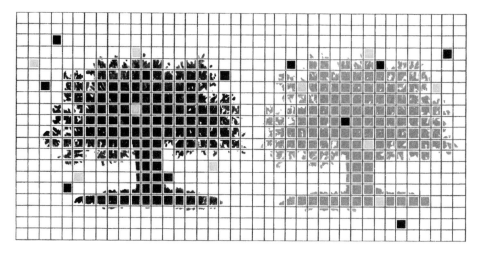

We have all encountered the TRUE/FALSE test that is performed as a basic part of all computer programming. In C, the if-else statement sequence performs this type of testing, as do the various looping mechanisms. A TRUE condition is evidenced by a value that is other than zero, while the FALSE condition is represented by a value of zero. Therefore, the TRUE or FALSE condition is finite within the language itself.

In conceptualizing artificial intelligence, we must deal with less finite conditions that will eventually equate to (or be equated to) TRUE or FALSE. In this conceptualization, the only kind of absolute TRUTH is one that is implied by the premise on which it is predicated. Expressed mathematically, we can say that if the premise is that X is equal to Y, and that Y is equal to Z, then X must be equal to Z. This is an absolute truth within the boundaries of the premise that X = = Y and Y = = Z.

If either of these premises are untrue, then the absolute truth may also be untrue. Therefore, all absolute truths are those that are implied. For instance, if a reliable survey shows that every fiftieth person in a fixed population has a cold, and the total fixed population numbers 50,000, then it is logical to state that there are 1000 persons in this population that have colds.

Naturally, the accuracy or absolute truth of the various implications can be challenged. In artificial intelligence fields relating to expert systems, the premise is the more important aspect, because the accuracy of the truth is predicated upon it.

We human beings have become adept at arriving at truths based upon incomplete premises. Some of us are quite good at building truths from this incomplete, or questionable, data. Those who are good at it are often referred to as expert in their fields. Others may be called soothsayers, charlatans, or "gifted". More often, one is said to have a "knack" for arriving at mostly correct conclusions from a mere smattering of premises. In expert systems programming, it is necessary to find out more about this "knack". This usually equates to the field of *statistics*.

The measured probability of a premise being true is called *statistical inference*, and its roots go back for centuries. In examining a premise, we must first examine the objects upon which the premise is based. In other words, if the premise states that a throwing die has a one-in-six chance of landing on any other side, we must take a look at the die to see if that premise is logical. In this instance, we see that the single die does indeed have six different sides. When thrown, the premise states that any side has a one-in-six chance of turning up. Therefore, it is logical to state that there is a one-in-six chance of any particular side turning up. This premise can be proven to a fairly high degree by throwing the die several thousand times.

Using the computer, it is very difficult to arrive at a "chance" occurrence via programming. Certainly, random number generators abound, but these are anything but producers of truly random numbers. In fact, if the algorithm used to produce these supposedly random numbers is known, then each and every number can be calculated in advance, just as the computer calculates them in advance. These then are actually pseudo-random number generators.

One might wonder what a discussion on chance, and the occurrence of random or pseudo-random events, has to do with artificial intelligence in expert systems. The answer is "quite a lot." After all, we humans, who are said to possess "true" intelligence (as opposed to the artificial type), calculate the odds on random events occurring every day of our lives. If we must drive downtown to buy groceries and be back by a certain time, we immediately judge such chance occurrences as a traffic jam, the store or stores most likely to be the least crowded, etc. All of these judgments are based upon certain premises that we have garnered through past experiences. And the "survey" or sampling of data upon which such premises are based may not have any direct connection with the task at hand.

For instance, if you are in a strange town for a week or so, and must do some grocery shopping, you will visualize this event. In other words, you will formulate a very good idea about what this shopping trip will entail. You will get your information about local traffic based upon what you have seen since entering this town. If you really haven't garnered any traffic information from this particular locality, then you will probably proceed on the premise that it will be the same as other similar localities you have visited. You would probably allow yourself a bit of extra time based on the fact that you have incomplete data. This series of logical exercises would continue on through your choice of market, selection of a shopping cart, choice of products, etc.

Now, this may seem like an exercise in the obvious, but in order to successfully program many aspects of intelligence, it is very necessary to clearly define on a step-by-step basis just what intelligence is. In this example, intelligence involves the capability of dealing logically with inexperienced occurrences based upon data garnered from similar occurrences. This also involves a calculation of the odds. We calculate odds every day, but we do this so naturally that most of us don't know we do it.

THE LAWS OF CHANCE

Using dice as a further example, let's examine some of the attributes of chance as a preparation for discussing the Laws of Chance. These laws, of which there are four, were developed by Galileo and mathematically explain much of what we know, almost instinctively, about simple odds today.

Proportionate Law

A throwing die has six faces. When it is thrown there is equal possibility of it falling with any face up. As previously discussed, the odds of any one face appearing are one-in six. Galileo's proportionate law, his first law, states this. However, this doesn't mean that if we throw the die six times, then all six faces will have appeared. As a matter of fact, the odds on this occurring are astronomical. However, if we make more than six throws (in multiples of 6), the proper proportions should begin to materialize. If we throw the die 6000 times, then each of the six sides should have appeared face up close to 1000 times. The higher the number of throws, the closer we come to unity for each face.

Using Turbo C, we can quickly arrive at a pseudo-random number routine that will quickly test this theory. There are two functions within Turbo C that we can start with. They are rand( ) and srand( ). The first function returns a random integer value ranging from 0 to 32767. The srand( ) function re-seeds the random number generator.

If you are confused about the term "seeding" the generator, just remember that rand( ) returns pseudo-random numbers via a mathematical routine. The numbers are no more random than is the square root of 4, but the complexity of the generator formula makes it impossible for a human being to determine any "logic" in the numbers sequence. The "seed" is simply a value that is initially worked through the pseudo-random generator formula. A different seed at the beginning of a run of random numbers will result in a completely different set of supposedly random numbers. If we used the same seed on every run, then the pseudo-random number sequence would always be the same.

For our purposes, all we want is a pseudo-random number range of from one to six. This corresponds to the faces of a single die. The C function in FIG. 3-1 is written in Turbo C and will return a random integer value within this range. This is a simple routine that is used elsewhere in this chapter, and in this text. Without going into detail at this point in the discussion, the function simply gets integers from rand( ) on two different calls, and divides the second into the first. The result is a floating point value that is assigned to a double variable. This same value is also assigned to an integer variable—therefore the fractional portion of this division is truncated.

Now the integer value is subtracted from the floating point value. The end result is the fractional component which serves as our random number between zero and one. This value is multiplied by six and added to one before being assigned to an integer variable. The end result is a

Fig. 3-1. This function returns a random integer value.

```
rand6()
{
    double a;
    int x;

    srand(seed);

    x = a = (double) rand() / rand();
    a -= x;

    x = a * 6 + 1;

    return(x);

}
```

pseudo-random number between one and six. A more detailed discussion of how this function works is provided elsewhere in this text.

Now that you have the random number routine that you want, it is necessary to write a program, shown in FIG. 3-2, that will allow for a proper demonstration of random values and the percentage of chance occurrences that will call this function. The program in FIG. 3-2 calls the previously discussed rand6( ) function and keeps count of the number of

Fig. 3-2. This program is called to demonstrate random values.

```
main()
{
    int r[6], x, y;

    r[0] = r[1] = r[2] = r[3] = r[4] = r[5] = 0;

    printf("input an integer value of from 1 to 30000\n");
    scanf("%d", &x);

    srand(x);

    for (y = 1; y <= 15000; ++y) {
        x = rand6();
        switch(x) {
            case 1:
                ++r[0];
                break;
            case 2:
                ++r[1];
                break;
            case 3:
                ++r[2];
                break;
            case 4:
                ++r[3];
                break;
            case 5:
                ++r[4];
                break;
            case 6:
                ++r[5];
        }

        printf("%-8d%-8d%-8d%-8d%-8d%-8d%-8d\n", y, r[0], r[1], r[2], r[3], r[4], r[5]);
    }
}

/* Source code for rand6() goes here */
```

times each number from one to six appears. The count value is displayed on the screen along with the number of "throws" that have been made. This, of course, is really the number of times the loop cycles. The switch statement within the loop simply reads the value in x which is the return from rand6( ) and increments the matching integer array value.

This array, r, is comprised of six elements numbered r[0] to r[5]. Each of these element values is initially assigned a value of zero. This is absolutely mandatory, because auto variables in C may assume any initial value upon declaration. On each pass of the loop, a printf( ) function displays the count in the integer array. The switch statement allows us to avoid a long line of if - else / else - if / else constructs, as in:

```
if (x == 1)
     ++r[0];
else if (x == 2)
     ++r[1];
else if (x == 3)
     ++r[2];
else if (x == 4)
     ++r[3];
else if (x == 5)
     ++r[4];
else
     ++r[5];
```

The use of the switch statement complex is more expressive. However, there are more efficient ways to handle the same construct. The switch statement tree could be modified in the following manner:

```
switch(rand6()) {
     case 1:
          ++r[0];
          break;
     case 2:
          ++r[1];
```

. . . etcetera. Because the return from rand6( ) is an integer value, it may be directly evaluated by switch and need not be assigned to variable x as before. Of course, we can be even more efficient and avoid the switch altogether as in:

```
for (y = 1; y <= 15; ++y) {
     ++r[rand6() - 1];
     printf("%-8d%-8d%-8d%-8d.
```

. . . etcetera. This last is the most efficient, but its intent may be hidden from C programmers who are just beginning to grasp this language. The subscript of the array (the named element) must be specified as an integer value. Rand6( ) returns an integer value of from one to six. Array r has six elements named with subscripts of from zero to five. Therefore, the return from rand6( ) minus one names the array element to be incremented. This is exactly what this construction accomplishes. All three examples do the same thing, but the last one uses a far more efficient method.

Such efficiencies and shortcuts are part of what makes C such a versatile language. However, this same attribute adds to the difficulty of learning this language.

With this program, you can see the count sequences getting closer to each other as the number of "rolls" increases. This is not the best example of a pseudo-random number generator routine, and it will generally tend to favor rolls of one and six. However, the idea is represented because large differences in the faces that have turned up tend to become equalized as the count continues. This tends to support the premise that any single face of a die has an equal chance of turning up.

With this test of the premise, we can state that the equal chance rule is a truth. It has been proven to our satisfaction mathematically, although we have used a computer program to make things a bit easier. I have tested this premise using far more elaborate pseudo-random number generator algorithms that are too complex to be useful in this discussion. As the rolls count upwards above 100,000, unity is almost reached in many instances. In other words, the difference in the number of times each face turns up becomes a very small fraction of the whole.

The discussion up to this point has gone through a lot of complexities in order to state the obvious. It's easy to see that if a die has six faces then any single roll will offer the same opportunity for any of the six to land upright. This would also apply to the flip of a coin, where any single flip can result in only one of two occurrences: heads or tails. By rewriting the random number generator algorithm to return values of one or two, the flip can be mathematically reproduced.

Additive Law

Assuming that we have proved to a reasonable degree that there is a one-in-six chance of any particular side of a die turning face up, let's move on to another premise that will indicate the probability of any of two sides of the die landing face up. This particular premise is addressed by Galileo's third law of chance which is called the additive law.

This law states that whenever there is the possibility of more than one result, then the probability of alternative results within a single occurrence is the sum of the individual probability. Put more simply: if there is a one-in-six chance of one particular die face turning upward, then there is a two-in-six chance of any of two faces turning upward.

For instance, the chance of rolling a six with a single die is one-in-six. This same ratio holds for any other single face. This was addressed by the previous premise. However, the chance of rolling a six or a two is two-in-six. This might better be stated as being a one-in-three chance of rolling any one of two die faces.

We are dealing here with ratios, but we are more accustomed to calling them fractions. Therefore, the chance of any one face appearing in the roll of a single die can be expressed as:

1 / 6

whereas the chance of any one of two faces appearing in a single roll can be expressed as:

1 / 6 + 1 / 6

or

2 / 6

or

1 / 3

Again, this applies only to a single die or any other object or event that offers the possibility of six different, and equally probable, results.

With this in mind, the chance of any one of three die sides turning face up on a single roll is:

1 / 6 + 1 / 6 + 1 / 6 = = 3 / 6 = = 1 / 2

In other words, there is one chance in two that any one of three sides of the die will turn face up on any one roll. The odds are 50:50 and become higher as we move upward through 4, 5, and finally 6 faces. The odds on any side of six faces turning up on a roll are unity or 1:1 or 1 / 1.

If all of this talk about odds and die faces seems to be obvious, you may be right. However, most of us are more accustomed to calculating easy odds such as this on more of an instinctive basis as opposed to a mathematical basis. Because artificial intelligence programming will require strict adherence to certain mathematical principles, it is necessary for the potential AI programmer to be able to define these apparent "instincts" in terms of mathematics, or lists, or some other form of expression that is convenient to representation via the C programming language. Unlike LISP, PROLOG, and other list-based languages, C is more mathematically or object based. C language deals with the same sort of objects that most computers do such as numbers, characters, and the memory addresses of these objects.

Now, while we all know that there is an equal chance that any one of six die faces will turn up on a single roll, most of us have never expressed this mathematically. Some readers may even have programmed simple dice roll games in BASIC or some other language without ever having found it necessary to predict odds mathematically. Usually, the random numbers generator statement or function common to any language used for this purpose has been utilized to (pseudo-) randomly arrive at the face values. No mathematical computations were necessary, save for the conversion routines (demonstrated earlier) to arrive at a random number in the range of values (one to six) desired.

The discussions in this book, and most other books on expert systems and AI programming principles, deal more with representation of concepts via universally accepted and recognized computer language constructs than with any other single subject. It is most important that we, as AI programmers, be able to express human-like thinking concepts in terms of the language in which we have chosen to program, than to have a great mastery of the particular language. LISP is often thought of as THE language of artificial intelligence. However, a thorough and professional programming knowledge of this language in no way prepares a person for AI programming unless the conceptual aspects of AI have also been taught.

If these concepts are mastered, then any language will suffice for AI applications, although some languages will make this task far easier than others. As was mentioned earlier, a surgeon's scalpel is absolutely necessary for surgery, but possessing one does not make a person a surgeon. A computer language is absolutely essential to write artificial intelligence programs, but mastering one does not make a person an AI programmer.

Multiplicative Law

We now know about some of the odds affecting the roll of a single, six-sided gaming die. Let's move on to dice and the odds that result from doubling the possibilities on an independent basis. We now have two sets of probabilities to deal with. The odds are exactly the same as discussed previously regarding the individual faces on each of the die. In other words, there is a one-in-six chance of rolling a four with one die, and a one-in-six chance of rolling a four with the other. However, when we must combine these odds to make predictions on what the "pair" will do, the mathematics become a bit more complex.

Fortunately, Galileo arrived at his fourth, or multiplicative, law that addresses this combination of odds. It states that whenever an object or event can have more than one result (any of which have an equal chance of occurring), the probability of getting a particular combination of results in more than one trail will be the product of the individual probabilities.

This law can address the simultaneous throwing of dice or the consecutive two throws of a single die. Either way, the combined odds are the same and are the product of the individual odds.

Using a specific example, we can further explore this fourth law. Let's calculate the odds on rolling two sixes. First of all, the odds on this face turning up on any one die are:

1 / 6

Because we are dealing with two dice, we use the product of the individual odds, or:

1 / 6 * 1 / 6

Therefore the possibility of getting "boxcars" is:

1 / 36

Out of 36 rolls, one of these should result in double sixes. Now, what are the odds of rolling a 6 and 4, or the odds of rolling a 3 and 2? The answer is the same:

1 / 36

Therefore, we can state that the odds of rolling any particular pair of faces when throwing dice is one-in-36. These odds would also prevail when calculating the results of rolling a single die two consecutive times.

We can return to Galileo's third, or additive, law to predict the possibility of any two or more combinations of faces turning up during a single roll of dice. As an example, calculate the odds of a single roll turning up a six and four, or a three and one. The odds are mathematically stated in the following manner:

(1 / 6 * 1 / 6) + (1 / 6 * 1 / 6)

or

(1 / 36) + (1 / 36)

or

2 / 36 or 1 / 18

There is a one-in-18 chance of rolling either combination. This should come as no surprise as there was a one-in-36 chance of rolling one specific pair. Therefore, the odds of success are doubled when two combinations are named.

Revising these figures slightly to mathematically explain the flip of a coin, the probability of the coin coming up heads or tails is 50:50 or:

1 / 2

By flipping two coins at once, the probability of any particular combination turning up is:

1 / 2 * 1 / 2

or

1 / 4

This relationship would hold true when rolling two pairs of dice, and would be stated as:

1 / 6 * 1 / 6 * 1 / 6 * 1 / 6

or

1 / 1296

This means that when two pairs of dice are rolled simultaneously, there is a one-in-1296 chance of rolling a specific combination. Technically, there is just as much chance of rolling four sixes as there is four ones, a one, two, three, and four or any other combination thinkable. The reason for this is that there are 1296 possible combinations, any one of which has an equal chance of occurring.

Instead of continuing to increase the number of dice we use for this discussion, let's switch to a standard deck of playing cards that number 52 without the jokers. The chance of drawing a particular card from the shuffled deck is:

1 / 52

owing to the fact that there are a total of 52 cards, any one of which has just as much chance to turning up as any of the 51 others. The chance of drawing a King of Hearts then is one-in-52. Now, what are the chances of drawing a King of Hearts *or* a Queen of Clubs. To calculate these odds, we return to the additive law which states that alternative results are calculated by summing the probabilities of each individual occurrence.

Because the probability of any single card turning up is one-in-52, the chance of either of two cards being drawn is stated as:

1 / 52 + 1 / 52

or

2 / 52 or 1 / 26

This tells us that the odds of either of these two cards turning up are twice that of drawing only a single specified card, or one-in-26.

Finally, the odds on drawing a certain combination of cards from the single deck would be:

1 / 52 * 1 / 52

or

1 / 2704

This means that there is one chance in 2704 draws that a specific two-card combination, such as a Queen of Clubs and a King of Hearts, would be drawn together in two successive draws. These are pretty fair odds, greater than rolling four sixes in a single throw of two pairs of dice. If we want to go to astronomical odds, consider the possibility of drawing a particular 52 card combination. In other words, you predict in advance the first 52 cards that would be drawn from a shuffled deck of 52 cards. The probability would be stated as:

One in 52 raised in the 52nd power

or

A Lot More Than Most Personal Computers Can Calculate

The reason for all of this attention to the odds is that these mathematical exercises are a fine introduction to sample taking and sample analysis—two of the tenets of certain branches of AI programming and cognitive scientific programming. Because we humans make assumptions based upon certain, almost automatic, odds calculations, it should not be surprising that certain fields of artificial intelligence research depend upon the same calculations.

Now, if the term "calculating the odds" sounds too unscientific to you, then simply think of this "science" as statistical analysis. That's what these discussions have entailed since the start of this chapter.

Before proceeding, let's discuss one more aspect of calculating probabilities of dice rolls or coin flips. Taking the latter as the easiest example to explore, what are the possibilities of a coin flip? Most people will aver that it has to be heads or tails. Indeed, a previous discussion in this chapter made this same assumption.

However, there is a third possibility that rarely occurs to anyone. Instead of landing heads up or tails up, the coin could land on its edge and remain balanced in this position. The odds on this happening are very nearly incalculable, but are probably one in many millions. It is good to know that the odds of this happening are so slim, because from a practical standpoint, this condition need not be planned for. However, it is also important to be able to pick out such anomalies when programming artificial intelligence applications. The truly good AI examples often plan for such rare contingencies, although most of these will not be as obscure in possibilities as a flipped coin landing edge up.

Ignoring the possibility discussed above, we can then safely say that a coin flip is a binomial event. This simply means that only two results are possible within the practical realm of probability. Practically speaking, the coin will always land heads up or tails up. Any other result is so far out of the realm of possibility as to be completely ignored.

Most of the higher animals are sexually binomial, being either male or female. Again, the odd androgyne or hermaphrodite is normally of such rarity as to be statistically ignored. We can even say that all numbers other than zero are binomial regarding sign or polarity, as they are either negative or positive in value.

In various aspects of calculating probabilities, it is often advantageous to arrange a binomial group or orchestrate an occurrence that offers a binomial result. There is even a Binomial Formula that deals specifically with binomial samplings. Previous discussions have skimmed the surface of probability predictions for certain binomial events. For example, if we want to know the probability of flipping a coin five times and ending up with heads on each of the five flips, the multiplicative law states that the odds are:

$(1/2) * (1/2) * (1/2) * (1/2) * (1/2)$

or

$1/32$

There is one chance in 32 that this series will occur. There is the same chance (1 / 32) that any of the 32 possible combinations will occur.

This multiplicative formula is great when dealing with a fairly small number of events, but the binomial occurrences add up to a lot of work when the number of events exceeds 25 or so.

It is for such occurrences that the binomial formula is provided. The formula is progressive and changes with the number of trials. If we assume that p equals the probability of an event occurring, and q is the probability of the single alternative occurring (as in the flip of a coin), then the formula for one trial is:

pow(p, n)

This means that the probability of getting heads (for example) on a single toss or trial is:

1/2 raised to the power of 1

or

1 in two

The formula for two trials (i.e. n == 2) is:

pow(p, n) | (n/1 * pow(p, n - 1) * q)

or

pow(.5, 2.0) + (2/1 * pow(.5, 1.0) * .5)

This equates to:

.25 + (2 * .5 * .5)

or

.25 + .5

This binomial formula consists of "terms". Each term predicts the possibility of a certain occurrence. For each trial, there is a different term. The above formula means that there is a one-in-four chance (.25) of flipping two "heads" during two trials, and a one-in-two (.50) chance of flipping one head and one tail. The first ratio is garnered from the first term, which is:

pow(.5, 2)

The .5 value represents the value of p which is the same as the fraction or ratio 1 / 2. This means there is a one-in-two chance of heads turning up. Because we are dealing with only one trial here, the value of variable q (which is the alternate event occurring) is not necessary. The second term is represented by:

(n/1 * pow(p, n - 1) * q)

The final value of .5 illustrates that when either event has an equal possibility of occurring, there is a one-in-two chance of two trials producing one of each event.

We can derive from this formula that the probability of coming up with two tails during two flips is exactly the same as that of coming up with two heads, or one-in-four.

By taking this last probability into account in our formula, we arrive at the following formulae:

> One Trial   pow(p, n) + pow(q, n)
> Two Trials   pow(p, n) [(n/1 * pow(p, n – 1) * q) + pow(q, n)

Each of these formulae have different terms to describe different trial numbers. All of them will eventually equate to the number one. This means that the possibility of any one of all of the probabilities occurring is unity—or certain. Taking the one trial formula as an example, and again using the flip of a coin as a test, we know that the probability of the flip resulting in either heads or tails is 1 / 2 or .5 . Therefore, the probability of the flip turning up heads is .5, and the probability of it producing tails is also .5 . Therefore, p = = .5 and q = = .5 . By working this through the binomial formula for one trial, you arrive at:

> pow(.5, 1.0) + pow(.5, 1.0)

which equates to:

> .5 + .5

or

> 1

Using the two trial formula, you get:

> pow (.5, 2.0) + (2 * pow(.5, 1.0) * .5) + pow(.5, 2.0)

which equates to:

> .25 + .50 + .25

or

> 1

If you want to take three trials into account, the binomial formula is:

> pow(p, n) + (n/1 * pow(p, n – 1) * q) + (((n * (n – 1))) /(2 * 1))
> * pow(p, n!2) * pow(q, 2.0)) + pow(q, n)

Again, this expression will always equate to one or unity when all terms are added together. Looking at the above formula, the first term describes the possibility of flipping heads (for instance) on each of three trials. The chances are one-in-eight. The second term describes the probability of flipping heads twice during three trials. This can also be described as the possibility of flipping two heads and a tail during three trials. The third term describes the probabilities of flipping 1 head and three tails in three trials and the fourth and final term provides the probability of flipping three tails during three trials. All of these probabilities add up to 1/1, because any one of these possibilities will actually result during any three flips of a coin.

C LANGUAGE PROBABILITY FUNCTIONS

You may be thinking, at this point, that this is all well and good, but how do we go about putting all of this into a C program or function. Certainly, committing a standard fixed formula or equation to a C program is quite simple. However, the binomial formula will always work out to unity, so we are not looking for the end results of this formula. Rather, we are looking for the results of a certain term or combination of terms. Also, this formula is not fixed. It is progressive and builds in complexity as the number of trials is increased.

Assignment

Write a C function that will take full advantage of the binomial formula just discussed.

Problems

- Formula is progressive.
- There is a need to return values of each term.

The C function in FIG. 3-3 has been named binomial) and will return the probability calculation for any number of trials. This formula does not answer all of the aspects of the original assignment, but it offers a good beginning. The binomial formula is used to return a single value which can be described as the probability of a single result being returned for a given number of trials. For instance, the probability of heads being flipped ten times in ten tries.

The binomial formula becomes more and more complex as the number of trials is increased. In this function, a value of -1 is returned if the value of n is less than or equal to 0. This indicates an error condition on the part of the user in that a zero or negative number of trials has been incorrectly fed to the function. When the trial number is one or two, direct returns are incorporated using the first two terms in the binomial

Fig. 3-3. The binomial( ) function returns a probability calcualation.

```
double binomial(n, p, q)
double p, q;
int n;
{
    int x, y;
    double t, mu, pow();

    if (n <= 0)
        return(-1);

    if (n == 1);
        return(pow(p, (double) n));
    if (n == 2)
        return(n * pow(p, n - 1.0) * q);

    y = 1;
    mu = (n * (n - 1));
    for (x = 2; x < n; ++x) {
        t = (mu / (x * y)) * pow(p, n - (double) x) * pow(q, (double) x);
        y *= x;
        mu *= (n - x);
    }

    return(t);
}
```

formula. For three terms and higher, a for loop is used to loop through to the correct term, altering the values of y and of mu during each cycle. These values increase as the number of trials is increased—thus their values are additive.

When the proper number of loop cycles has been completed, the value in t is the correct probability for the number of trials initially input. Notice that this function has been declared double. This means that the value it returns is a double precision floating point number. Any program or function that calls binomial( ) must also declare this function a double precision type. The following calling program illustrates this usage:

```
main()
{
    double p, q, binomial();
    int n;

    printf("Type the value of p, q, and n\n");
    scanf("%lf %lf %d", &p, &q, &n);

    printf("%lf\n", binomial(n, p, q));

}
```

Truth, Chance and Statistics   49

This program allows the user to input the various values of p, q, and n. It then calls binomial( ) from within a printf( ) function. This is perfectly legal, as binomial( ) will equate to the double precision value of its return after execution has taken place. Note that binomial( ) is declared a double precision type in the declaration line of this calling program.

Again, this function is a good starting example, but it does not allow for the examination of each term in the overall formula. As illustrated, this function is only useful for determining the probability of one of two events occurring during each and every trial. To look at other possibilities that are also contained within this formula, it is necessary to work out a method where each term is returned as a separate value.

The only way to do this is to use a double precision array to hold the result of each term. We already know that if we specify ten trials, then this will necessitate working through ten terms plus an eleventh one which will hold the probability figure for the alternative event occurring during each and every trial. Because the function discussed already does this, it is only necessary to "capture" the results of each of these terms and pass these values back to the calling program or routine.

Obviously, we can't use the return( ) statement in C to return more than a single value. Therefore, it will be necessary to pass a variable from the calling program that can be written to by the function. In this case, the variable in question must be a double precision floating point array, one that is dimensioned to allow for the maximum number of anticipated trials plus one more. Additionally, this array must be a pointer, because we want the function to write the term contents to a place in memory that can be accessed by the calling routine. It is therefore necessary to declare the array within the calling program and then pass its memory address to the function. With the memory address, the function can then write the term contents to the correct place in memory and, upon returning to the calling program, our array will contain that data.

The program in FIG. 3-4 is just a little more complex than the one just discussed. It is only a slight modification of the previous function, allowing it to return each term instead of only one. Again, this is simply a rework of the original function that allows a pointer to a double array to be passed. This function then fills the array with each term of the formula. A typical calling routine might be written as shown in FIG. 3-5.

In this example, ar is declared a double array of twenty elements. This dimensioning was arbitrarily chosen. If more terms are to be worked, then a larger array is needed. Also, variable b is declared to be a pointer of type double. Variable b is later assigned the memory location of

Fig. 3-4. This bonomial ( ) returns each term.

```
binomial(z, n, p, q)
double p, q, *z;
int n;
{
    int x, y;
    double mu, pow();

    if (n <= 0)
        return(-1);

    *z++ = pow(p, (double) n);
    if (n == 1) {
        *z++ = pow(q, (double) n);
        return(0);
    }

    *z++ = n * pow(p, n - 1.0) * q;
    if (n == 2) {
        *z++ = pow(q, (double) n);
        return(0);
    }

    y = 1;
    mu = (n * (n - 1));

    for (x = 2; x < n; ++x) {
        *z++ = (mu / (x * y)) * pow(p, n-(double) x) * pow(q, (double) x);
        y *= x;
        mu *= (n - x);
    }

    *z = pow(q, (double) n);

    return(0);

}
```

Fig. 3-5. Here is a typical calling routine.

```
main()
{
    double p, q, *b, ar[20];
    int n, x;

    b = ar;

    printf("Type p, q, n\n");
    scanf("%lf %lf %d", &p, &q, &n);

    binomial(b, n, p, q);

    for (x = 0; x <= n; ++x)
        printf("%lf\n", ar[x]);

}
```

the array via the b = ar expression. Now, pointer b points to the address of the first element in ar. As before, the user must input the values for p and for q as well as for n. The binomial( ) function is called with the necessary arguments. Upon return from binomial( ), the array ar now contains each of the terms in the binomial equation. The simple for loop reads each of the terms contained in the array.

You will notice that return( ) statements are still used throughout this new binomial( ) function. These return values simply indicate relative success or failure of the function. As before, an inappropriate trial value n will result in a −1 return. This value is a standard error value for various standard functions within the C programming language. On the other hand, correct values for n will result in the formula being worked properly.

Once the array has been loaded, the function is exited via a return(0) statement. This return value of zero can be read by the calling the function or program to make certain that the binomial( ) function is indicating a correct functioning with the argument values provided. Again, this is only an indication that the function has correctly completed its execution with arguments that are appropriate. The actual results from this binomial( ) function are contained in the double precision floating point array that served as its first argument when binomial( ) was called.

It should be understood that pointer b merely carries the memory location or address of the start of the array. With this address, the function knows where to write information to the memory locations set aside for storage to array ar. Many beginning C programmers will simply pass the array to functions and this won't fly. Remember, a C function cannot write to variables contained within the calling routine or program unless the memory address of these variables is known. The only way to do this is to pass the memory address directly to the function via pointers. This is exactly what has been done in the latest binomial( ) function.

If you want to avoid the pointer operations just described, there is a handy way to accomplish this using a global array. A global variable is one that is declared outside of any function and is therefore known to any and all functions. An example of this usage is in FIG. 3-6

It can be seen that double precision floating point array ar is declared ahead of main( ). Because the declaration was not local to the main( ) function or to any other, this becomes a global array that can be directly accessed by any function. Because the declaration was made ahead of all functions, it is not necessary to declare ar extern. But if a global variable is declared after certain functions that may need to use it (i.e. just before

Fig. 3-6. Here is an example of global variable usage.

```c
double ar[20];
main()
{
    double p, q;
    int n, x;

    b = ar;

    printf("Type p, q, n\n");
    scanf("%lf %lf %d", &p, &q, &n);

    binomial(n, p, q);

    for (x = 0; x <= n; ++x)
        printf("%lf\n", ar[x]);
}
binomial(n, p, q)
double p, q;
int n;
{
    int x, y;
    double mu, pow();

    if (n <= 0)
        return(-1);

    ar[0] = pow(p, (double) n);
    if (n == 1) {
        ar[1] = pow(q, (double) n);
        return(0);
    }

    ar[1] = n * pow(p, n - 1.0) * q;
    if (n == 2) {
        ar[2] = pow(q, (double) n);
        return(0);
    }

    y = 1;
    mu = (n * (n - 1));

    for (x = 2; x < n; ++x) {
        ar[x] = (mu / (x * y)) * pow(p, n-(double) x) * pow(q, (double) x);
        y *= x;
        mu *= (n - x);
    }

    ar[x] = pow(q, (double) n);

    return(0);
}
```

binomial( )), then that global variable must also be declared extern from within any functions that will need to have access to it.

Because ar is known to both main( ) and to binomial( ), it may be freely read from, or written to, by both. This is exactly what is being done in the last example. Basically, all that has been done within the function is to replace the pointer with the array.

Progressive formulas such as the one just discussed are usually transported to C programs or functions with relative ease. It does take a bit of forethought and planning to handle these transportations in an "elegant" manner, as opposed to a "brute force" approach where each step is laboriously programmed verbatim. In each of these examples, a brute force method is used to return, or to write, probabilities based on one or two trials. After this point, however, a for loop is used to allow the formula to progress. Many different progressions are allowed via a single program line. Variable y is assigned an initial value of 1(one) and then is incremented within the loop. Variable mu contains the initial n * (n − 1) value and is incremented by its current value times (n − x) on each loop pass. You can readily see the efficiency of this type of programming in that this same expression represented by mu would be written in a brute force manner for either trials as:

n * (n − 1) * (n − 2) * (n − 3) * (n − 4) * (n − 5)

However, this progression is handled automatically from within the for loop by incrementing mu via the expression:

mu * = (n − x)

which is C language shorthand notation for:

mu = mu * (n − x)

This same method is used for incrementing the value of y which is divided into the mu sequence. Using the above brute force example as a guide, the value contained in y would be written in a brute force manner as:

7 * 6 * 5 * 4 * 3 * 2 * 1

Therefore, the combined mu/y equivalent would be:

(n * (n − 1) * (n − 2) * (n − 3) * (n − 4)
* (n − 5)) / 7 * 6 * 5 * 4 * 3 * 2 * 1

And this is just for the eighth trial sequence. This formula is different for seven trials and for nine as well.

When committing complex mathematical formulas to a C language program (or for that matter, any computer program), it is necessary to fully understand the workings of the formula. Progressive formulas, such as the one under discussion, cannot simply be copied verbatim to the program as can many simpler formulas. It must be understood that a progressive formula changes structure on each progression. It is not a fixed formula then, but a series of different but related formulas that combine to produce the desired results.

The following combination tables illustrate the results from several different "runs" using either the last two binomial( ) functions:

/* p = = 0.500000   q = = 0.500000   n = = 3 */

    Term 1 = 0.125000
    Term 2 = 0.375000
    Term 3 = 0.375000
    Term 4 = 0.125000

/* p = = 0.500000   q = = 0.500000   n = = 8 */

    Term 1 = 0.003906
    Term 2 = 0.031250
    Term 3 = 0.109375
    Term 4 = 0.218750
    Term 5 = 0.273438
    Term 6 = 0.218750
    Term 7 = 0.109375
    Term 8 = 0.031250
    Term 9 = 0.003906

/* p = = 0.900000   q = = 0.100000   n = = 6 */

    Term 1 = 0.531441
    Term 2 = 0.354294
    Term 3 = 0.098415
    Term 4 = 0.014580
    Term 5 = 0.001215
    Term 6 = 0.000054
    Term 7 = 0.000001

/* p = = 0.995000   q = = 0.005000   n = = 4 */

    Term 1 = 0.980150
    Term 2 = 0.019701

Term 3 = 0.000149
Term 4 = 0.000000
Term 5 = 0.000000

Notice that when the value of q becomes very small (as in the last two examples), it becomes more difficult to express this alternate factor as a viable fraction or decimal value. The same would be true if the value of p were to be reduced to a very small quantity. The first two tables were produced using the coin flip figures from earlier discussions, i.e. there is an equal 1/2 or .5 chance of the main event or the alternative event occurring. However, the last table yields very little usable data because q's value is very very low. This last series of trials might have been used to predict the probability of a flipped coin landing on an edge instead of a face during four trials. The initial value of p might be an estimate of the possibility of the coin landing on either face (an almost 100% probability). The value of q would then be a statement of the possibility of the coin landing on its edge (a very minute quantity).

You can see from the various terms produced by the binomial( ) function that the probability of the coin landing on a face during four trials is 0.980150. The chance of the coin landing on its face three times during four trials (and once its edge) is 0.019701. The odds of the coin landing on a face two times and landing on an edge two times in a total of four tries is a scant 0.000149. The chances shrink even more when you read the possibility of the coin landing on its edge three times and on a face only once in four trials, and you end up with 0.000000 (no chance at all). This is the same figure you get for the last term that states the probability of the coin landing four times on its edge in each of four trials.

Poisson's Probability Formula

I have stated that there is little usable data available when the value of q (or of p) becomes very small. Although the above example is just an example, it does serve to illustrate this point. The figures yielded by this run are certainly not exactly correct, even assuming that the starting values of p and of q are correct. (In fact, they were arbitrarily chosen for this discussion and bear no relationship whatsoever to the accurate percentage of face/coin probability.) Though it is true that four flips of the coin will not yield a single landing on an edge and, furthermore, that four flips will certainly not result in the coin landing on an edge four times, there is more than a zero possibility that this could occur. We know that the coin does have a possibility of landing on an edge. You may have never seen it happen, but you can conceded that it could. Therefore, there is a possibility that it could happen more than once and, in fact, even four times in a row.

It is quite easy to calculate the basic odds for a single trial when we are talking about such rudimentary examples as flipping a coin. There is a fifty-fifty chance. However, something as ethereal as a flipped coin landing on an edge instead of a face involves something more than simple mathematics. For such an example, we are entering the area of isolated occurrences. We humans tend to think of such occurrences as "God's will," "a freak accident," "a billion to one shot" or whatever you like.

The chance of such events occurring is so remote as to defy most "predictive" mathematics. This last expression is one I have *coined* to describe the math used, for instance, to predict the one-trial probabilities of a coin flip. You know that each side has a fifty-fifty chance of turning up, even though we also know that there is a very, very, very remote possibility of the coin landing on its edge. This last possibility is so remote as to be ignored. By ignoring such remote chances, the predictive math is quite easily handled. Here is a sequence of thinking processes that go into such math:

1) The coin must land on a face
2) There are two faces
3) Both faces are equal in width, weight, etc.
4) There is an equal chance (50-50) of either face turning up

True, you could calculate the surface area of the edge and compare it with the surface area of the faces. However, you would also have to calculate other factors such as the balance of the coin, curvature of the edge, etc. However, by discarding the edge, the predictive math sequence shown above is quite easily applied, just as it is for the roll of a die or for the drawing of a single card from a deck of 52. The latter example is more finite than the first two. When you draw a single card from a deck of 52, then that card has to be one of the 52. However, when you flip a coin, the result can be either a face or an edge. When you roll a die, the result can be any one of six faces or an edge.

However, as a human being you are aware of the possibility of the occurrence of isolated events which can throw all standard prediction awry. Because you often take these occurrences into account, it is necessary to have the mathematical capability of doing the same thing in order to delve further into artificial intelligence applications.

Now, how do you go about getting the mathematical percentages for the occurrence of an isolated event, which might better be called a random happening. You have already learned that the criteria for such events happening is often immeasurable from a human standpoint. There are just too many factors to consider, some of which you may not even be aware.

However, there is an excellent meter for getting a handle on the occurrence of isolated events. It is so obvious as to go unnoticed in this discussion—so far. This meter is simply the number of times this event has happened in the past measured against the number of trials that have occurred in the past.

If you have flipped a coin 10 million times and had the coin land on an edge ten times, then you can say that the odds of this happening again are one-in-one million. This is easy. However, suppose you have not flipped a coin 10 million times. Assume also that you have heard from two different acquaintances that they have personally witnessed a coin land on its edge on one occasion. While you don't know how many trials this represents, you do know that this random occurrence has happened at least twice. Believe it or not, there is a formula which is a modification of the binomial formula just discussed that is used to predict the reoccurrence of random events, based upon the number of times such events have occurred in the past.

This is known as Poisson's Probability formula and is written as:

$$e^{-m} + \frac{m}{1} \times e^{-m} + \frac{m^2}{2 \times 1} \times e^{-m} + \frac{m^3}{3 \times 2 \times 1} \times e^{-m} + \frac{m^4}{4 \times 3 \times 2 \times 1} + e^{-m} \ldots$$

Here, e is equal to the base of the Naperian logarithms, which is 2.7183. This is a modification of the binomial formula and is divided into terms. The first term expresses the probability of a certain random event occurring no more times (i.e. zero reoccurrences). The next term defines the odds of it happening once more. The following terms express the odds of two, three, four, etc. more occurrences.

The m variable in this formula states the number of known past occurrences. The more accurate the value of m, the more accurate will be the probability return.

As you may have suspected, this formula is quite easily written into a C function. Because this is a modification of the binomial formula, the C function in FIG. 3-7, named poisson( ), is a modification of binomial( ). You will again notice how this progressive formula is committed to a simple for loop that is used to increment the value of y and to determine the power to which m is raised on each loop pass.

Fig. 3-7. This is poisson ( ), a modification of binomial ( ).

```
poisson(z, i)
double *z;
int i;
{
        int x, y;
        double e, m, em, pow();

        e = 2.7183;
        m = i;
        em = pow(e, -m);

        if (m <= 0)
                return(-1);

        *z++ = em;
        *z++ = m * em;

        y = 1;
        for (x = 2; x < 10; ++x) {
                *z++ = (pow(m, (double) x) / (x * y)) * em;
                y *= x;

        }

        return(0);

}
```

Fig. 3-8. A typical program that calls poisson ( ).

```
main()
{

    double *b, ar[10];
    int i, x;

    b = ar;

    printf("How many times has this event occurred in the past?\n");
    scanf("%d", &i);

    poisson(b, i);

    for (x = 0; x < 8; ++x)
        printf("Chance of reoccurrence %d times is %lf\n", x, b[x - 1]);

}
```

A typical program that might call this function is shown in FIG. 3-8. This program then becomes an artificially intelligent fortune teller of sorts. However, the future predictions are based on supposedly sound mathematical probabilities, and not on the guesstimates of a human being.

SUMMARY

This chapter has examined a sampling of formulas, techniques and thinking patterns associated with statistical rules that have been with us for centuries. While it is important to be aware of many of these techniques for various types of AI programming in expert systems, it should also be understood that one direction of AI leads away from pure statistical analysis, which really addresses probabilities. More and more the trend is to do away with probabilities, avoid them entirely, and to concentrate on methods that bring about answers or results that are more absolute in nature.

Regardless of the direction(s) your AI pursuits lead, it is most important that you understand the methods by which mathematical formulas are committed to the computer program, and specifically how to program such formulas to best advantage in the C programming language. This chapter has shown some of these methods, and should enable you to continue in this same vein toward the more complex methods of statistical representation and sampling.

4

Game Playing

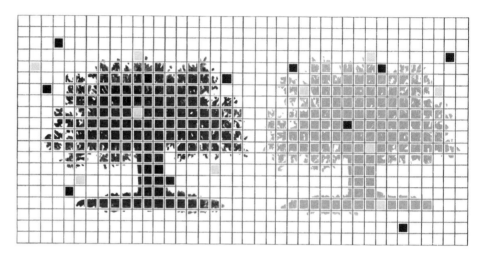

"Games, the innovations of the highly intelligent." Some ancient Greek philosopher can probably be credited with that quotation, however it is not entirely accurate. Today, we do recognize that games and game playing are not restricted only to human beings, nor for that matter to the higher order of primates. Game playing would seem to be mostly limited to mammals, however, with the more highly cognitive games played by the higher order of this class.

As infant human beings, we have been taught to think via a series of games. One of the first games an infant learns is "Pat-a-Cake". This outwardly simplistic rhyme involves not only cognitive exercise, but also develops motor skills and the initial coordination of the motor/cognitive orientation necessary to become what is termed "a thinking human being."

Among humans, games seem to have been developed out of a need to exercise our "thinking devices" during times of boredom when there is nothing to tax our thinking abilities, and during times of stress. In the latter, these thinking devices have been overworked and need to be refreshed. Just as the Tibetan peoples run in order to rest bodies that are fatigued from walking (a different set of muscles is used), thinking games that may require intense mental acuity are able to relax a mind already fatigued from application of the same mental powers targeted at another problem.

Anthropologists have learned about the mental, social, and psychological make-up of ancient peoples, long extinct, by studying the games they played and handed down to their distant descendants.

Many of the games we humans play are mathematical in nature, even though many of them may not seem so. Indeed, mathematics is a language that is informally taught long before any type of ritualized schooling has taken place.

Can you remember playing Hide and Seek as a child? As I recall, it was necessary for seekers to hide their eyes and recite a "meaningless" rhyme before seeking to find the scattered "hiders". If you were quite young, then you used the abbreviated form of this rhyme which was "Ten, Twenty, Thirty . . . Eighty, Ninety, One Hundred. Here I Come, Ready Or Not." When you progressed to the "senior" level of this game, then you could impress your playmates with the expanded rhyme that went "Five, Ten, Fifteen, Twenty . . . Eighty, Eighty-Five, Ninety, Ninety-Five, One Hundred. Here I come, Ready Or Not."

Even today, I can remember reciting these "rhymes" long before I realized what they represented. So ingrained through social interaction were these game poems that I was midway through the third grade when I realized that they were mathematical progressions. From years before I had been reciting the multiplication tables for ten and five, respectively, and never realized it.

I struggled through the multiplication tables in steps of two, three, and four. It was only when studying the tables in steps of five that I learned that I already knew them by heart. I quickly realized that I also knew the tens tables as well. This may seem like a trivial discovery but, believe me, it was a revelation! I think this experience forever changed the way I felt about mathematics. Its vestiges remain with me today.

Humans are mathematically oriented. Mathematics is a language. It is a language that describes what is known about the physical universe. It is a universal language, highly different and separated cultures have arrived at quite similar forms of mathematics. There are distinct dialects of mathematics, but they are all readily understood by persons who have made a study of this highly descriptive language.

Mathematics is called the universal language. When humans finally make contact with intelligent extraterrestrial beings, the language used for communication between them will probably be mathematics. This assumption is based upon the ability to readily decipher the various dialects of mathematical systems that have been discovered among different cultures on this planet. It is a fact that our present "world" mathematics is highly "human" oriented. When speaking on a cosmic scale, this humanization of our mathematical language makes it far less than a truly universal language. However, the universal concept of mathematics may be a correct one.

Stating that our systems of mathematics are highly humanized is readily demonstrated by most basic mathematics found on this planet: they're all base 10. Hexadecimal, octal, and binary math are more a product of advancements in mathematical proclivity than they are a natural part of a basic number system used for practical applications. (However, there are apparent examples of systems using other than base 10 in several ancient cultures.)

Why base 10? The reason is simple and should be immediately obvious to humans. Count the digits on each set of extremities on the human body and you arrive at 10. Primitive man began his mathematical operations by counting the fingers on one hand. He progressed over the eons to two hands and, even later, to the maximum of ten dirty toes on his unshod feet. It is no wonder that we humans would tend to lean toward a system of numbering that uses the base ten. This is the base that our physiological structure has dictated.

Nor is the mathematics humans currently possess a fixed, unchanging language. Mathematics will change whenever something radically new is discovered about the physical universe. At present one plus one is equal to two. However, if the situation is discovered where, given a set of circumstances, one plus one is equal to something other than two, then an adjunct to the current mathematics will come into being that will describe this condition.

MATH AND MUSIC

It has been said that anything and everything the human mind can conceive can, eventually, be expressed in terms of mathematics. Taken quite literally, this would mean that a walk in the country could be described in all detail, sight, sound, smell, touch, etc. in purely mathematical terms. I won't dispute this assertion, but I do strongly agree that the current mathematical language has not been developed to even a small percentage of the size and complexity needed to allow for such a description.

However, our present mathematics is highly developed enough to take the place of other types of language. To start this element of the discussion, think of a musical manuscript. The various symbols form a graphic representation of sounds. A musical manuscript, then, is a chart of sounds. Indeed, musicians refer to such manuscripts as "charts" —perhaps a more descriptive name. These charts are really several graphs rolled into one. A bar chart is formed by the musical staff.

The positions of markers (notes) on these horizontal lines determine the frequency of the tone. The divisions of these charts are called "bars". The note marker takes one basic form, an oval. If the oval is hollow, this represents one mathematical unit of duration (the length of time the indicated frequency is to be sustained). If the oval is filled in, this represents a division of this basic duration. If a vertical line is added to one side of this oval, the division is multiplied. If the vertical line is terminated in an upward flag, the division is multiplied again. Two flags: a further division. Of course, these durations are not given in absolutes but in percentages or fractions of some unit. The whole unit is determined by the time signature which, in turn, is referenced against a tempo designation. This combination yields most of the factors necessary to produce the correct frequency of tones of the correct duration and repetition.

All of these musical attributes could be described in purely mathematical terms. Instead of the graphic math chart that currently comprises a musical score, the notes could be specified by frequency, just as the note duration could be described in fractions of a universal time unit. Indeed, computers are quite capable of such musical performances by outputting tones of specific frequencies and durations as are dictated by their programming. Such programs are purely mathematical in nature.

This is not to say that a human musician can be directly replaced with a machine. No two musicians will play the same piece of music the same way, even though both may be reading from the same musical score. There is another element to music or, more accurately, to the performance of music that is incorporated when human beings are added to the chain. Musicians often use the musical manuscript as a guide to the performance, as opposed to using it as a "strict" set of instructions on how a particular piece is to be played.

The end product that is the output of a musical performance by a musician will include a great deal of what musicians refer to as a special "feel" for that particular piece. This feel is also referred to by other names such as style, phrasing, etc. It is this element that differentiates from a purely mechanical output of various frequencies at various time durations, and from what we call music.

This seeming departure into the music world still relates to the original discussion on mathematics as a language. Though you can accurately describe the frequency and duration of musical notes via a standard musical manuscript, or even via a long list of frequencies in kilohertz and durations in fractions of a second, you have more difficulty in musically describing the subtle innuendoes of performing music that has been called a musician's "feel".

Certainly, a musical manuscript will include special notations that have to do with the amplitude (volume) of the tone, progressions of amplitude (when to get loud and when to get soft), and various other easily definable aspects of audible sounds. But it is more difficult to indicate on paper, using concrete mathematical methods, how the musician "bends" a note (intentionally produces a certain note in such a way that it lies between two bonafide musical notes). This center note is not a bonafide note at all, because it lies between the frequency ranges of two actual notes. As such, it cannot be explicitly notated in a musical manuscript. Its actual frequency must lie somewhere between the bonafide notes that lie on either side of it in the musical frequency spectrum. But no two musicians will produce the same "middle note", so it is somewhat of a variable—not a constant. How is this stated mathematically?

The frequencies of the notes could be specified on either side of this desired middle frequency as high and low ranges, and incorporate a random number generator to produce a value that lies somewhere between them. However, the musician performing this piece of music doesn't arrive at this "blue note" in a random fashion. Rather, the musician bends the note up or down until it "feels" right.

What is really needed is to express, in mathematical terms, the "feel". But what is this feel? The same musician may do it one way in one performance, and then do it differently in one that follows an hour later. The feel referred to here is the human element that cannot be programmed on a computer, and cannot be written in concrete mathematics. One reason for this is that even musicians cannot define this feel. They are incapable of explaining why the piece was handled in one way during a particular performance, and another way in a later one. Certainly, you can assume that this "feel" has to do with the inner emotions of the musician at the time. Furthermore, this can be directly related to the amount of sleep the musician got the night before, what the musician had for breakfast, how the musician interacted with friends and relatives, whether or not the musician had a happy childhood, etc.

The musician, the musician, the musician—that's the key. The performance has to do with the musician, and not as much with the concrete structure of the musical piece. The variable and undefined human element has entered the picture. And, at present, we cannot program the entire human element into a computer—nor even a significant part of this mystery element.

The mathematics and the computers that can emulate a part of this mystery element are now available. If emulation is the sincerest form of flattery, then many of today's forays into artificial intelligence flatter human beings. How is this emulation accomplished? The answer is: in many ways.

In our above musical example of a musician bending specified notes slightly off frequency in response to the "feel" at the time, emulation might be easier than is outwardly obvious. Remember, the emulation referred to involves the sound of the final performance and not the thinking processes, conscious or subconscious, that have caused the human to perform in a specified manner. In other words, if you can mathematically express a certain musical piece, or program its performance on a suitably equipped computer in a manner that closely emulates the human performance, it doesn't matter if this emulation resulted in a type of "thinking" process that is completely removed from that gone through by the human performer. Put another way, if it sounds like the real thing, then it must be the real thing, regardless of how you got it to sound that way.

Before relating just how this emulation can be accomplished mathematically in a computer program, we must first determine our field of control or influence. In this example, take one bar of music that comprises four notes played over a duration of about one second. This is all we are concerned with in this discussion.

Assume that a musician plays the first two notes exactly as written during 100 performances. However, the third note is "bent" a little during all performances, and the fourth note is bent sometimes and not played exactly as written at other times. At this juncture, we have a professional "sampling" in the form of the 100 recorded performances. We will assume that this one second interval from each performance has been measured and the low and high frequency range of that bent note are garnered from these measurements.

Just as I restricted this discussion to a small portion of the total performance (one bar), you also have to realize that the object of this exercise is not to emulate human performance of this one second of music, but to emulate this human's performance: the human whose 100 performances have been sampled.

The first two notes in this bar are no problem. We have already ascertained that they are played exactly as written. These two notes can be programmed by frequency duration, etc. taken directly from the musical manuscript. The third note, the one that is always bent a little sharp or flat by the performer, is the first problem. For the sake of argument, say that the note ranges from 503.8 hertz to 520.76 hertz. This corresponds to the frequency that lies between B and middle C in the musical scale. No bonafide note lies between these two notes, because they are a half step apart. C-flat is the same as B-natural and B-sharp is the same as C natural. In this range, B-natural lies at a frequency of 493.880 hertz, and middle C is at 523.250 hertz.

During the 100 performances, the musician played this third note in a manner that bent it to within the frequency range listed above. The first thing to look for is a pattern to this bending. Did the musician bend it to one frequency more than another? If the answer is "no", then you can set up the random number generator mentioned earlier to choose a frequency at random each time the program is executed. If the answer is "yes", the random number generator is still used, but a preference is given to the frequency that is more often repeated. In this case, we might program a random number routine that would output a value of from 1 to 100. If a particular frequency was output, say one-fourth of the time, by the performing musician, then you might add a routine whereby any random value between 25 and 50 would result in this particular frequency being output. All other random numbers outside of this range would result in other frequencies.

This type of mathematical routine, when applied to a computer program, would artificially replicate the live performance of this three-note portion of the musical piece. However, you still have to deal with that last note that is sometimes played as written and sometimes played in the "bent" manner of this exercise.

Again a random generator would be used that would address the generation of bent notes within the proper range and, on other occasions, output the manuscript note. No problem here. Now, have you done all you can to artificially mimic the live performer's phrasing of this one second segment of music?

There are other factors yet to be considered. To really get sticky about this whole matter, a dedicated mathematician would look for a relationship between the two variables, i.e. notes three and four. Does the attained frequency of note three seem to have any direct bearing on the frequency of note four? Comparing the two might reveal that when note three is bent to a particular frequency, note four is always played as the manuscript dictates. It's just as likely that this isn't the case, but assuming it is, you can arrive at a further means of replicating the human performance.

In actual practice, one is not likely to find this type of direct relationship in comparing something as ethereal as a human musical performance. However, a trend might be found. This might take the form of the fourth note being played to manuscript tolerance whenever note three falls close to a certain frequency. Or, note four is played to tolerance fairly often when note three falls within a certain frequency range. The percentage of such a trend or sequence could easily be built into a random number routine.

If you want to pursue this exercise (which is ridiculous from all but a sophistry standpoint) to maniacal ends, a relationship between performances might be sought. Here, you would be looking to see if the way one performance was handled seemed to have any effect on the way to follow—if the first 25 performances showed any marked deviations from the next 24 or the last 25, etc.

Think of all the cognitive energy that has been spent in discussing this simple, little one second of music. However, once the performance of music was boiled down into a purely mathematical entity, the problem of performing it in a style that is bordering on basic human mimicry was less difficult. Of course, the big bugaboo is emulating human thinking processes that are not so easily defined. These are the subconscious feelings, intuitions, and snatches of genius that set humans apart from machines. These can't, as yet, be programmed because they are not well enough understood.

A musical exercise was chosen for this discussion, because it is easy to boil down musical performances into purely mathematical progressions. If musical performances considered only of the absolute output of sounds in accordance with the written set of instructions for musical manuscripts, then machines would probably have been doing all of the concerts in the world. This is not the case, as a musical manuscript serves only as a general guideline to be interpreted, to large and small extents, by the various conductors and performers. Nor is such "do it by rote" mechanics the case in most types of functions where human beings are involved.

At one time, artificial intelligence experts concentrated on how human beings think and tried to develop algorithms that would allow a computer to go through the same processes. This is still the case with certain aspects of AI but, more and more, AI as it relates to the expert system in today's society is less concerned with the process and more concerned with the product. Another way of putting this would be to state that when an expert system is asked a question, the prime concern is to output the correct answer every time. It doesn't make any difference if human-like thinking processes have been incorporated into the program to arrive at this answer. Of course there are purists who are still striving for the ultimate: a machine that thinks the way we do. Perhaps someday.

SIMPLE EMULATION OF HUMAN THOUGHT

One aspect of artificial intelligence programs involves duplicating the identifiable human thinking processes where possible. Some will argue that this is what all of artificial intelligence is about, but this is a highly debatable point, as are many other aspects of the concept of machine intelligence. In any event, certain types of human actions and reactions can be easily identified and as easily emulated through computer programming. However, many others are not as easily identified. And even when they are, committing these actions or mental processes to a computer program are seemingly impossible.

As a crude example, suppose you wish to establish whether an animal is a mammal or a reptile. By asking a few simple questions, the needed data can easily be gathered and a decision made. The first question might well be:

Does this animal nurse its young?

If the answer is yes, then it must be a mammal. However, if the answer is no, then it must be some other type of animal—though not necessarily a reptile. The next two questions might be:

Is this animal cold blooded?
Does the animal have scales?

If the answers to these questions are both yes, then you can determine that this animal may indeed be a reptile.

A simple computer program can be written to emulate these specific operations and to check the answers. The program might be written as shown in FIG. 4-1. This extremely simple example is very limited, but it does provide a very useful example of a program that emulates the human thinking processes used to determine if an animal is a mammal or a reptile.

The system breaks down when the programmed questions are unknown. For instance, if it is not known whether the animal nurses its young, then it will be necessary to answer more questions. One must also consider the possibility of receiving wrong answers to questions and to determine that such answers are indeed erroneous from correct data acquired through more questions.

Fig. 4-1. This program determines whether an animal is a mammal.

```c
main()
{
    int x;
    char a, b, c;
    printf("Does this animal nurse its young?\n");
    scanf("%c", &a);
    if (tolower(a) == 'y') {
        printf("This animal is a mammal\n");
        exit(0);
    }
    else {
        printf("Is this animal cold blooded?\n");
        scanf("%c", &b);

        printf("Does this animal have scales?\n");
        scanf("%c", &c);

        if (b == 'Y' && c == 'Y') {
            printf("This animal is a reptile\n");
            exit(0);
        }
        else
            printf("This is neither a mammal nor a reptile\n");
    }
}
```

The above example contains only three possible outcomes: mammal, reptile, or neither. If the problem is expanded to identify mammals, reptiles, insects, plants, fungi, metals, gasses, minerals, etc., then the thinking processes must be made many times more complex.

This simple program begins to illustrate just what an expert system is, and how it would work. It does its job by "setting switches" that are represented here by the if - else constructs. Based upon known criteria, "if this is so and that is so and this isn't so, then the outcome must be so". That's basically how an expert system works, although we will learn more about this field of artificial intelligence in a later chapter. For now, let's move on to some game playing and replicating the human thinking process in a manner that is very, very much like the real thing!

There are times when the human thinking processes can be closely mimicked, seemingly in most major details. This especially applies to the way humans might tackle a mathematical problem. Computers are mathematical machines and most languages are outwardly mathematical in nature. Languages most associated with AI programming seem to be object or list oriented, but these too can be resolved into purely mathematical components. C language is outwardly mathematical in nature.

As an example of a direct emulation of the human thinking process, I have chosen a game program that should be familiar to all readers. It seems that nearly every book written between 1977 and 1983 that dealt with general BASIC language programs obtained a version of this program. While it went by many names, the most popular was "GUESS MY NUMBER". The concept is simple. The computer picks a whole number between 0 and 100 at random. The user tries to guess this number by inputting guesses. The computer says whether the guess is high or low. The idea is to arrive at the correct number while making the least guesses possible.

The C language equivalent of this program is shown in FIG. 4-2. This example is written in Turbo C. Other C environments may contain

Fig. 4-2. "Guess My Number!"

```
main()
{
    int guess, actual, x;
    double y;

    guess = -1;

    puts("Type any positive integer");
    scanf("%d", &x);

    srand(x);          /* Reseed random number generator */
    x = y = (double) rand() / rand(); /* Get random value */
    y -= x;    /* Remove any whole number value */
    actual = y  * 100 + 1;
    x = 0;

    puts("I am thinking of a whole number of from 1 to 100");
    puts("Input your guess");

    while (guess != actual) {
        scanf("%d", &guess);
        if (guess < actual)
            puts("Too Low. Guess again");
        if (guess > actual)
            puts("Too high. Guess Again");
        ++x;
    }

    Printf("That's It!!! You got it in %d guesses.\n", x);

}
```

different functions to return a random integer number and to reseed the random number generator. Here, srand( ) reseeds the random number generator, while rand( ) returns a random number that is an integer. This is converted to a double precision floating point value by calling rand( ) again and dividing this second random integer into the first. Notice that the (double) cast operator is used to coerce the first random integer to type double so that the divide operation will result in real number division instead of integer division. The result from this division operation is assigned to two variables simultaneously.

However, variable y is of type double and x is of type int. This means that y is equal to the actual value of the division operation, while x is equal to only the integer portion of the same operation. If the result is less than 1, then x is equal to zero. If the divide operation results in a value of 4.77653, then y will be equal to this value and x will be equal to 4. The next line subtracts x from y (y -= x) which means that y is now equal to only the fractional portion of the original divide operation. Therefore, y will always be equal to a value that is greater than zero and less than 1. This is then multiplied by 100 and the result added to 1 to arrive at a random integer ranging from 1 to 100 when assigned to integer variable, actual.

This simple game program is not an example of artificial intelligence. However, you will observe the thinking used by the human player to begin to address the task of programming some identifiably human responses.

This program uses three int variables in the following manner:

guess = players guesses
actual = actual random number
x = number of guesses made

Within the while loop the player's input is compared with the hidden value at random by the computer. Based upon the value of the player's guess, prompts are displayed indicating whether the guess is high or low. When guess = = actual, the loop is exited and the number of guesses is displayed on the screen before program termination.

Now, place yourself in the player's position. The computer has chosen a number at random that lies somewhere between 0 and 101 (i.e. a value of from 1 to 100). What would be your first guess? The best first guess would be 50. This will place the actual hidden number in one of two quadrants. The first encompasses all numbers from 1 to 49, while the other quadrant contains those numbers from 51 to 100. What does this do? First, it eliminates half of the possible numeric choices. Second, it allows the player to accurately determine the next best guess.

Remember, the object of the game is to get the hidden number while making the fewest guesses possible.

Assume that the mystery number is 61. With an initial guess of 50, the computer will prompt that the guess is too low. Therefore, you know that the number lies in the range of 51 to 100. The next best guess would lie at the halfway point between these two values, or 75. To this guess, the computer would respond with the "Too High" prompt.

You now know that the mystery number lies somewhere between 50 and 75, therefore the next best guess will be at the midway point between these values which is 62 or 63, depending on which way you round. The prompt is again "Too High" so the number must lie between 50 and 62. The next guess would be the midway value of 56 which elicits a "Too Low" computer prompt. The next midway guess would then be 59—also too low.

Through the process of elimination, you now know that the hidden number is either 60 or 61. Either of these values would constitute a "best" next guess. If the one chosen is incorrect, then the next must be the secret number.

This exercise should make it easier to write a program that will mimic the thinking processes of the human player. What have you learned from this game "talk through"?

1) The first best guess lies at the midway point within the possible range of values.

2) The next best guess lies at the midway point within the range of values that were not eliminated by the previous step.

Mathematically, the formula for arriving at best guesses is:

bestguess = high − ((high − low) / 2)

or

bestguess = low + ((high − low) / 2)

Remember, the high or low values change with each guess. Through the process of an ever-narrowing range of possible values, the hidden number is derived.

The procedure is very simple, so simple in fact that it involves only a single, simple mathematical formula. Here, the human thinking process is such that pure mathematics can be used to describe it. This also means that it can be emulated through a computer program, a program that will seem to think in a manner similar to the human player faced with solving this puzzle.

The C program in FIG. 4-3 reverses roles from the previous one. Here, the human is asked to think of a number. The computer will then guess this number based upon human prompts of "Too High" or "Too Low". In other words, the human assumes the computer's role and the computer the role of the human in comparison with the last program.

The program in FIG. 4-3 simply uses one of the two possible formulas discussed earlier that constitute the best guess method used by the human player. If you assume that the "talk through" of how the original game was played by the human is accurate, then this last computer program very closely emulates this player's "thinking" processes while trying to determine the mystery number.

Explained simply, this program assigns to variables high and low the high and low range values. Variable guess is initially assigned a value of high / 2 which is the first best or midrange guess. After the loop has been entered, the values of low and high are altered based upon the user supplied information as to whether a best guess is high or low. The formula

Fig. 4-3. This program plays "Guess My Number!".

```
main()
{
    int low, high, guess, count;
    char c;

    puts("Think of a whole number of from 1 to 100");
    puts("When you have a number in mind, press <ENTER>");
    scanf("%c", &c);

    count = 0;
    low = 0;
    high = 100;
    guess = high / 2;

    while (low != high - 1) {
        printf("Is your number less than %d (Y/N)\n", guess);
        c = getch();
        if (c == 'y' || c == 'Y')
            high = guess;
        else
            low = guess;

        guess = high - ((high - low) / 2);
        ++count;
    }

    printf("Your number is %d. It took me %d guesses.\n", low, count);
}
```

discussed earlier for determining a best guess is found near the end of the program in the form:

guess = high - ((high - low) / 2;

On each pass of the loop, count is incremented by 1 to allow for the total number of guesses made by the machine to be recorded.

These simple games may have been impressive during our beginning weeks and months of learning to program (probably in BASIC), but they seem quite inane to experienced C programmers. These are, at best, interesting exercises, but is this last game really an example of artificial intelligence?

The answer is yes! Admittedly, this is a very basic example of AI. But if you feel that it requires intelligence on the part of the human being to play the original game, then the computer's ability to emulate this same intelligence must be recognized.

As a further test, two human beings could play this numbers guess game, communicating via the computer keyboard and modem. Here, the computers would serve only as communications devices with one human typing messages to the other. Player A would think of a number from 1 to 100 and player B would try to guess this number, based on high or low clues from player A. If player B were suddenly replaced by a computer running the latter program, player A would probably not be able to detect the difference if the mechanics of the game were all that the two-way communication involved.

The above scenario could also take place without the advantage of human players. The players would be two computers, one running a program that would arrive at a random number between 1 and 100 and supply high/low clues to the second computer that would try to guess the number.

The program in FIG. 4-4 requires no human intervention once the game is begun. The guesses and responses are displayed on the screen purely for human observation purposes. Note that variables guess, high, and low are declared externally. Therefore, they are known and may be accessed by the calling program (main) and by the function named newguess( ). The initial values of these variables are established in the main program. These values are changed within the body of newguess( ). This latter function is a much shortened version of the last program under discussion and uses the high - ((high - low) / 2) sequence to arrive at new best guesses.

The main program obtains a number at random and calls newguess( ) each time a guess is to be made. This function arrives at the new guess based on the formula above, and on its only argument which is either

Fig. 4-4. This program plays itself at "Guess My Number!"

```
int guess, high, low;

main()
{
    int actual, count, x;
    double y;
    char c;

    printf("Press any key to reseed generator.\n");
    c = getch();
    srand(c);

    count = 0;
    x = y = (double) rand() / rand();
    y -= x;
    actual = y * 100 + 1;
    guess = 50;
    high = 100;
    low = 0;

    while (guess != actual) {
        printf("MY GUESS IS %d\n\n", guess);
        if (guess < actual) {
            printf("Too Low--Try Again\n\n");
            newguess("low");
        }
        else {
            printf("Too High--Try Again\n\n");
            newguess("high");
        }
        ++count;
    }

    printf("MY GUESS IS %d\n\n", guess);
    printf("That is correct. It took you %d guesses.\n", ++count);

}
newguess(a)
char a[];
{
    if (strcmp(a, "low") == 0)
        low = guess;
    else
        high = guess;

    high - ((high - low) / 2);


}
```

"high" or "low," and which is expressed as a char array. The global variable values are changed in accordance with the actions of newguess( ).

This program involves only one computer with the main program supplying the hidden numbers and the appropriate clues and the newguess( ) function supplying the "intelligent guesses. However, these two, discrete operations could be divided into separate programs, and executed on separate computers connected by modem. A human observing this interchange could not definitely identify either or both players as human or machine.

Of course, like any good debater, I can also argue the "other side" quite effectively. Suppose this numbers guess game were changed to a children's math game whereby the teacher might ask the student player to give the sum of 2 + 3. This is an even more mathematically finite example than the numbers guess game. Naturally any computer would be able to supply the answer. Is this any different from the numbers guessing game? Yes and No.

It can be argued that the computer's guessing a hidden number requires "logic" whereas simply performing a standard mathematical operation does not. Of course, if you did not know that 2 + 3 was equal to 5, but knew that 2 + 2 was equal to 4, then you might be able to deduce that 2 + 3 was equal to 5 by "logically" viewing it as (2 + 3) = 2 + 2 + 1. In general, you can say that the ability of the computer to detect a hidden number known only to the user is a more "human like" operation than is the performance of simple mathematical operations.

These arguments can, do, and maybe always will lead to many heated discussions into the wee hours of the morning. The big question is when do simplistic mathematical or logic operations become more than the sum of the whole. When do a combination of simplistic logic operations reach a level of complexity to be classified as an "intelligent" operation? That question has been answered many times, but only to the satisfaction of the one providing that answer. To others, another answer may be more highly regarded. To still others, the answer has never been found.

SUMMARY

The purpose of this chapter was to arouse your curiosity by showing some simple examples of how human thinking processes can be directly applied to a computer program. It should be noted, however, that artificial intelligence research is no longer heavily oriented toward copying these human processes. Rather, programs are being written and computers are being designed that will provide information, guidance, assistance, problem processing and other attributes that have traditionally been provided by human beings.

It is no longer a prime factor that the computer seem to think or even act like a human—only that it supply information in an understandable form when interacting with humans. However, the study of the human thinking processes, when applied to many problems, provides a starting point for adaptation of these processes or computer-equivalent processes in the effort toward development of practical expert systems.

5
Data Management for AI Systems

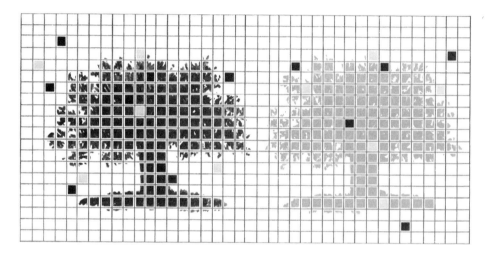

Many uses of artificial intelligence in expert systems involve the necessity of accessing vast amounts of data. In most instances, such data are stored on disk and accessed via standard filekeeping routines. This is especially true of most expert systems that combine sophisticated filekeeping and data base management with highly complex AI routines to access the needed data from a very large data bank or to write additional data to such banks. Because of the large quantity of data required, access times can be quite slow, especially when operating in the realm of the microcomputer.

Many expert systems make use of *ramdisks* which are simply large portions of memory that are set aside to store disk data in a format that fools the computer into thinking this memory is, indeed, a true disk drive. The latest versions of MS–DOS are equipped with a ramdisk driver, so such an installation is no problem, providing that the needed memory is available.

When using a memory disk of this type, standard filekeeping functions may be used to open, read, write, and append files just as though all information is being read from or written to a disk. However, instead of a slowly performing disk, the information transfer is taking place in memory, therefore access times are hundreds of times faster. Generally, all data is initially loaded from a true disk file or files into the ramdisk. When the program is exited, all new additions to the data base are rewritten to the disk file, thus preserving all information for the next time the expert system is used.

Although the ramdisk method of data access is very fast, it does create some problems for the programmer who must write the access routines using standard filekeeping functions. Because the available memory may vary from machine to machine and the required storage space will vary as well, it is difficult to efficiently establish an in-memory disk that is memory efficient and still adequate to meet the on-line storage needs of the user. There is the advantage of using familiar functions in arranging this data in what appears to be a standard file format. The other alternative is to load file data into large arrays and access it from there. However, this can be confusing and there are no standard functions for manipulating this data in file fashion.

To overcome some of these problems, I wrote a series of in-memory filekeeping routines that allow precise control of memory usurped for this purpose and still provide a note of familiarity to programmers through the use of equivalents of common file functions.

One of the beauties of the C programming language is the grouping of names of input/output functions according to data stream access. For instance, the printf( ) function directs its data stream to the monitor or standard output as it is more commonly called. Its sister function is fprintf( ) which directs its data stream to a file. Still another sister function is sprintf( ) which directs its stream to a character array. The same grouping can be found with gets/fgets, puts/fputs, getchar/fgetc, scanf/fscanf/sscanf, etc. As a beginning C programmer, it was easy to make the transition from the standard input/output functions to those used to address disk filekeeping, because they all work in a similar manner. The only differences lie in the direction of the data stream.

VIRTUAL FILEKEEPING FUNCTIONS

The special functions that are discussed in the remaining pages of this chapter were written to address the need for a very fast set of tools to access large quantities of data, stored initially in disk files. These functions were designed to be used comfortably by any programmer who uses their filekeeping equivalents that are a part of the standard C language function set. With these functions, you can quickly open a virtual file that is simply a RAM memory equivalent of a disk file. These memory files are opened, closed, written, read, and accessed in exactly the same manner as disk files, using functions that are immediately identifiable as an extension of the current sister functions already available in this language.

Whereas the standard disk file functions in C are given names that begin with the letter f, these special functions use the same names but replace f with the letter v for virtual. Using these functions should be quite natural. To open a memory file, the vopen( ) function is used, just as fopen( ) is used to open a disk file. The vopen function will require an extra argument that specifies the size of the file in bytes, but other than this, it is used exactly like fopen.

To close a memory file, vclose(fp) is used where fp is the file pointer returned by vopen. This set of special functions also contains other memory file equivalents of the standard C filekeeping functions set including vgets( ), vputs( ), vlink( ), vseek( ), vgetc( ), vputc( ), etc.

The following discussions will take you through the operation of each of these special functions. Many programmers will want to combine all of these into a single header file which might be appropriately named vio.h, the virtual equivalent of stdio.h. Others might wish to combine the vio.h file with stdio.h so that an entire set of filekeeping functions, disk and memory, may be addressed by one header file. Whenever the memory file functions are used, it is usually necessary to also do some actual disk filekeeping. That is, it is usually necessary to read data from a disk file already in existence, or to write data from a memory file to a disk file for permanent storage. Therefore, combining the two header files makes good sense.

Again, each of these functions in this tool set will be discussed on an individual basis. All of them should be combined to form a practical set of memory file functions that can be used with the same efficiency, comfort, and understanding as those sister functions which are an integral part of the standard C language library.

vfil.h

Using the memory file functions requires, at a minimum, the inclusion of a header file named vfil.h. The contents of this file are displayed in the listing that follows:

```
struct vfile {
    char *fiptr;
    long vfiloc;
} VFIL[20];

#define VFILE struct vfile
```

```
VFILE *v[20];
char *finame[20];
int fino = 0;
```

First a struct is declared and named vfile. It contains a string pointer named fiptr which stands for file pointer. A long variable is declared and named vfiloc which stands for file location. For reference throughout this discussion, fiptr points to the starting memory location of the opened file and vfiloc contains the offset into that file. In other words, when a memory file is first initialized (opened) for writing, fiptr points to the start of memory where this file is to be written. With each character written to the memory file, vfiloc is incremented by one. Therefore, vfiloc is used as a counting mechanism within the file while fiptr locates the beginning of memory set aside for the file.

Notice that this structure actually is an array of VFIL structures that can be used to open as many as twenty different files at one time. This header file also contains three external variables and a macro definition that makes declarations within programs that use the memory file tool set easy. The macro declaration allows VFILE to be used as a substitute for struct vfile, just as FILE is predefined in the stdio.h header file is −included with other C programs that use the standard filekeeping functions.

Caution: external variables are necessary in this header file. Therefore, no program that uses these memory file functions should make use of variable names *finame[ ], *v[ ], fino, etc. If there is a conflict here, then the variable and pointer names within this structure, and within other functions that address memory filekeeping, must be changed accordingly. As their names imply, *finame[ ] contains the names of the opened memory files and fino indicates the total number of files that are opened.

Because all of the memory file tools were designed to be contained within a header file that is included whenever they are needed, vfil.h can be thought of as a header file to a header file. More appropriately, if a programmer desires to package the memory file functions in a library file, the minimum header file just described must still be #included. This gives the programmer the option of deciding the most convenient manner of gaining access to the memory file functions.

You should realize that the structure just described is really an array of structures, and a maximum of twenty memory files may be opened at any one time (or more if you increase the array count shown here). Therefore vfiloc and fiptr may be called on to access many different files that are open simultaneously. The member-of-structure operator −> will be used to indicate which of the twenty possible structures are being referenced. This is better demonstrated in the discussions that are to follow.

vopen( )

The vopen( ) function is used to open a memory file for read, write or append. Its operation is identical to fopen( ), its disk file counterpart, but it does require an extra argument. The vopen function is used in a format of:

```
fp = vopen(name, mode, bytes)
```

where *fp and *fopen( ) have been declared VFILE pointers as in:

```
VFILE *fp, *vopen( )
```

In this example, name is the name of a memory file, mode is read, write, or append signified by "r", "w", or "a" in standard C fashion, and bytes is an unsigned integer which names the maximum file size. This unsigned integer is used as an argument to calloc( ) in the vopen function and is limited to 64K in size. The name argument is included to maintain convention as it is used with fopen( ). The file name is necessary when removing a memory file, because it serves as the argument to vlink( ), just as the file name is used as the argument to unlink( ) in the standard C function set.

Again, the only programming difference in using vopen( ) lies in including the memory file size. This is necessary, because a certain amount of memory must be reserved for access by the pointer that is returned by this function. This isn't necessary when opening disk files, because whatever is left unused on the disk is immediately available for such purposes. When dealing with memory files, things are a bit different and a specific amount must be set aside. Therefore, the programmer should know the maximum number of bytes that might be required for each opened file and specify these parameters accordingly. The vopen( ) function does check to make certain adequate memory is available for all requests and prints an "Out of Memory" error message when more memory has been requested than is actually available. This also causes program termination. This latter feature can be canceled by changing a few program lines. The vopen( ) function could just as easily return NULL when memory space is unavailable. The NULL could then be tested for in the calling program. FIG. 5-1 contains the sourse code for vopen( ).

Though it is not necessary to know exactly how vopen( ) works in order to use it successfully as a programming tool, this discussion will provide you with a quick "walk through" that may enable you to come up with other implementations which better suit your own, particular AI

Fig. 5-1. vopen ( ) opens a memory file.

```
VFILE *vopen(a, b, bytes)
char *a, *b;
unsigned bytes;
{
    char *calloc(), malloc();
    int i;

    if (strcmp(b, "r") == 0 || strcmp(b, "a") == 0) {
        for (i = 0; i < fino; ++i)
            if (strcmp(a, finame[i]) == 0) {
                v[i] = &VFIL[i];
                if (strcmp(b, "r") == 0)
                    v[i]->vfiloc = 0L;
                else
                    v[i]->vfiloc = (long) strlen(v[i]->fiptr);

                return(v[i]);
            }
    }
    else if (strcmp(b, "w") == 0) {
        v[fino] = &VFIL[fino];
        v[fino]->vfiloc = 0L;
        if ((v[fino]->fiptr = calloc(bytes, 1)) == NULL) {
            puts("Out of Memory");
            exit(0);
        }

        strcpy(finame[fino] = malloc(20), a);
        fino++;
        return(v[fino - 1]);
    }
    else
        return(NULL);

}
```

programming needs. The entire memory file function set was written in Turbo C (Version 1.5), but this code should compile successfully with any full range compiler. The functions are written for portability in that the calloc( ) memory allocation function is used as opposed to Lattice's getmem( ) which is often a more efficient means of memory allocation in a microcomputer environment. The standard memory allocation function, calloc( ), is UNIX compatible and, while not as efficient as other similar functions, is portable. User's of specific C compilers may wish to change calloc( ) in these listings to a compiler specific equivalent for improved memory allocation efficiency, assuming that portability is not a requirement. The calloc( ) function is used in this example as opposed to malloc( ), because it is desirable to allocate and clear memory (as calloc( ) does) rather that to just allocate memory. The calloc( ) function effectively allocates the desired contiguous bytes of memory, and then fills the block with NULL characters (zeros). This feature is needed to accurately detect the current end of file.

This vopen( ) function is passed three arguments which are the file name, mode of access and file size. The latter argument is only necessary when the file is being opened for a write operation. This argument may be deleted for read and append operations. Unlike disk files, memory files must always be opened for a write, loaded with information (presumably from a disk file), and then closed. Later they can be reopened for a read or an append. As a matter of fact, the vclose( ) function is included, again, just to maintain convention. As might be expected, memory files are always opened for read and write, regardless of the mode that is specified. However, the file must first be opened for write, because this is the mode that causes vopen( ) to set the memory file size.

When the function is first entered, strcmp( ) is used to test for a mode of read or append as is indicated by an "r" or "a" respectively. If this is the case, this means that the file has already been opened and loaded using a previous "w", therefore no memory has to be allocated. Make certain you understand this aspect of the function! You cannot open a file for reading that does not exist. This applies to any file, whether it be the standard disk type or one in memory. Unlike the fopen( ) function, a file that is opened for append which does not exist is not opened and results in an error. Do not open any file for append that has not previously been opened for write!

Assume that a file is to be opened for read. This is detected by strcmp( ) and a for loop is entered. This loop counts variable i from zero to the one less than the number of opened files. The finame[ ] array is read, looking for the identifying file name. Char pp in array v[ ] is then assigned the memory location of the correct structure in the array of structures. Assuming a read operation, the member-of-structure operator is used to assign v[i] – >viloc a value of zero. This constant is followed by "L" indicating that this is a long integer value as opposed to a standard integer value.

Again v[i] is assigned the correct structure in our array of 20 possible structures—one for each possible opened file. v[i] – >vfiloc is the member of this particular structure in the array of structures that contains the long variable vfiloc which indicates file position. This complex procedure has simply accessed the correct file through the appropriate structure and rewound it. The starting position in the file for the read is offset zero.

To go further, let's assume that a file is opened for a write. Here the else if expression takes over. A file opened for a write is newly created. First v[fino] is assigned the currently available file position. Next it is rewound in the same manner just described for the read file initialization. The next step uses the calloc( ) function to allocate the memory requested in the vopen( ) argument to this pointer. Should the memory not be available, an Out of Memory message is displayed and execution terminates.

However, assuming that everything is proper at this point, the memory is allocated, and the file name used with vopen( ) is copied to finame[ ] using strcpy. The fino variable is incremented by one so that the next request for a file creation will be assigned a new number and new array structure. The return statement hands the pointer to the newly created file back to the calling program.

For the sake of simplicity, a lot of protective features have not been included. When a request is made to open a memory file for a write operation, no check is made of the file name to see if it has been previously used. Therefore, it is possible to have two files with the same name. When an attempt is made to reopen any one of these, the first one created will be the one that is always opened. This can be corrected by inserting a for loop in the else if construct to test for the file name already being contained in *finame[ ] just as it is in the code that sets up an open routine for reads and appends.

An append operation is handled just like a request for a read, however the file is wound to the current file end instead of to the beginning. This line is found in the source code just prior to the first return statement.

The operation of vopen can be described as follows.

To detect a Read or Append:

1) Find file number
2) Assign proper structure
3) Wind file to proper position
   0 for read, end for append

To detect a Write:

1) Assign file number
2) Assign array struct
3) Initialize pointer
   (use calloc to allocate memory)
4) Make Copy of name
5) Return file pointer

As was mentioned previously, any memory file that is opened for a write operation may also be read or appended. This applies to all of the other file modes as well. For instance, a file can be opened for write, information from a disk file read into it, and then the memory file can be read without closing the file and reopening it for a read operation. This will require that the file be wound back to the beginning or, more appropriately, the file pointer must be reset to the beginning character in the file. Another function can easily accomplish the rewind and is discussed later in this chapter.

vputs( )

Now that a function has been presented that will open a memory file, it is necessary to arrive at others that can be used to actually write information to the memory file, or to read information from it. The next function is called vputs( ) and works like fputs( ) does for disk files. It writes a string of characters to an opened memory file. This latest function is used in a format of:

vputs(a, fp)

where a is a character array or string pointer and fp is the memory file pointer returned by vopen( ). The vputs( ) function actually writes strings a character at a time until the NULL character is encountered. It is a very simple function that simply writes the characters in the string to the sequential memory positions reserved for the file. With each character that is written, the value of vfiloc, which keeps track of the relative file position (i.e. the offset for writing the next byte), is incremented by one. This is identical to the method used by fputs( ) to write bytes to a sequential disk file.

To understand this operation a bit better, assume that the first string to be written to a newly opened memory file is "Computer/n". Assume also that this is contained in char array a[ ]. Because this is the beginning of the memory file, vfiloc is equal to zero or offset zero. Therefore, the letter "C" will be written at file position zero, and then vfiloc is incremented by one. The next letter, "o" is written at offset 1, because vfiloc is now equal to one. Again vfiloc is incremented and the progression continues until "Computer/n" is written to the file. When the write is complete, vfiloc is equal to 9. This means that the next write that is made to the memory file will begin at offset 9.

The source code for vputs( ) follows:

```
vputs(a, ptr)
char *a;
VFILE *ptr;
{
        while (*(ptr->fiptr + ptr->vfiloc) = *a++)
            ++ptr->vfiloc;
}
```

This function consists of a while loop that advances the file pointer a byte at a time as it advances the pointer position to the string accessed by *a. Notice that vfiloc or, more accurately, ptr – >vfiloc is used to get the offset and that this value is incremented by one on each pass of the loop. Don't be confused by the member-of-structure operator. Remember, ptr is a pointer to the memory file array opened for current use. Therefore, ptr – >vfiloc is the vfiloc variable contained in this array. Also, *(ptr – fiptr + ptr – >vfiloc) names an offset into the file.

To explain this in simpler terms, assume that a pointer identified as *g points to a character string equal to "Hello". Knowing this, *a = 'h' and *(a = 1) = 'e' and *(a + 2) = 'l', etc. This is the same notation used in *(ptr – >fiptr + ptr – >vfiloc). In other words, ptr – >fiptr names the file pointer while ptr – >vfiloc names the offset. Another way of looking at this is *ptr – >fiptr reference file position zero. By adding ptr – >vfiloc, an offset into the memory reserved for the opened file is obtained.

vgets( )

The reciprocal function of vputs( ) is called vgets( ) and it retrieves, or reads, a string of characters from a file. As is the case with fgets( ), the vgets( ) function reads a string of characters up to a number specified by one of its arguments, or until a newline character is encountered in the memory file it is reading. When a newline is encountered, vgets( ) replaces it with the NULL character /0. If the maximum byte-read value is reached before a newline is encountered,k vgets( ) simply terminates the character string with the NULL character. The format of vgets( ) is:

vgets(1, byte__num, fp)

where a is a char array or pointer, byte__num is an integer value specifying the maximum number of bytes or characters to read from the file, and fp is a memory file pointer returned by vopen( ).

Fig. 5-2. vgets ( ) reads a string of characters from a file.

```
vgets(a, x, ptr)
char *a;
int x;
VFILE *ptr;
{
      int ct = 0;

      if (*(ptr->fiptr + ptr->vfiloc) == '\0')
            return(NULL);

      while ((*a++ = *(ptr->fiptr + ptr->vfiloc)) != '\n' && ct < x) {
            ++ptr->vfiloc;
            ++ct;
      }

      ++ptr->vfiloc;
      *a = '\0';

      return(1);

}
```

The function in FIG. 5-2 first declares an integer, ct, with a value of zero. A check is made to see if the first character pointed to is the NULL character. This signifies the end of the file and a NULL is returned to the calling program. Assuming that this is not the case, the while loop is activated. This assigns to *a++ the sequential succession of characters read from the file. The loops tests for the occurrence of a newline character or of ct being equal to x. When either of these conditions prove true, the while loop terminates. On each pass of the loop, both vfiloc and ct are incremented by one. The first variable is keeping track of the file offset position. The second counts the number of characters read. Upon loop termination, vfiloc is incremented once more and the NULL character is tacked onto the end of *a. A return statement returns a value which is arbitrarily 1. This could be any value other than zero, the latter indicating a NULL or end-of-file return.

vwind( )

The rewind( ) function in C is used to reset a disk file pointer to the beginning of the file. The equivalent is also available in the memory file function set and is called vwind( ). This latter function is extremely simple, because all that is necessary is to reset vfiloc, the memory file offset variable to zero. The source code for vwind( ) is:

```
vwind(ptr)
VFILE *ptr;
{
     ptr->vfiloc = 0L;
}
```

Because vfiloc has been declared a long integer, it is reset to 0L. Once this is done, any calls to read or write the memory-file whose VFILE pointer was used as the argument to vwind( ) will begin at the start of the file.

vtell( )

In the standard C language function set, the ftell( ) function is used to return the position of the file pointer offset. This indicates the current offset in effect which is the same as the position into the file where the next character will be read or written. The memory file equivalent of this function is called vtell( ) and, like its standard function set equivalent, it returns a long integer. For this reason, it must be declared in the following manner by any program that calls it:

long vtell( );

C assumes that all functions return integer values, unless specifically told otherwise, as is the case with vtell( ). Because vfiloc indicates the current file offset, all vtell( ) has to do is return its value. The following source code reveals that it does just this:

```
long vtell(ptr)
VFILE *ptr;
{
     return (ptr->vfiloc);
}
```

This function consists simply of a return statement to pass the value of ptr->filoc back to the calling program. The only argument required by vtell( ) is the memory file pointer that is used to access the correct vfiloc variable from the array of structures. Remember, ptr names the desired structure in the array of structures and ptr->>filoc variable within the chosen structure.

vseek( )

To maintain strict control and access of files, it is mandatory that a function be provided that can move the file pointer offset to any specified file elements or bytes. In the standard C language function set, fseek( ) is such a function. In the memory file set of functions, vseek( ) does the same thing. This function is used in a format of:

vseek(fp, off, mode)

where fp is the memory file pointer returned by vopen( ), and off is a long integer value that specifies the offset value. The third argument is an integer value of 0 or 1 that indicates how the offset value is to be used. Like fseek( ) and lseek( ) in the standard C library, vssek( ) mode arguments indicate the following offsets:

0 - relative to beginning of file
1 - relative to current file position

With an offset value of 10 and a mode argument of 0, the offset will be to the tenth character from the beginning of the file. A mode argument of 1 would direct the pointer to the tenth character ahead of where the pointer was positioned when the vseek( ) call was made. The source code for vseek( ) is shown in FIG. 5-3.

The operations of this function should be self explanatory, but for beginning C programmers, a quick run-through is provided. The entire function consists of an if — else-if — else construct that tests the value of

Fig. 5-3. vseek ( ) moves the file pointer offset.

```
vseek(ptr, off, mode)
VFILE *ptr;
long off;
int mode;
{
    if (mode < 0 || mode > 1)
        return(-1);
    else if (mode == 0)
        ptr->vfiloc = off;
    else if (mode == 1)
        ptr->vfiloc += off;

    return(0)

}
```

the mode argument before proceeding. Remember, ptr-vfiloc is a long integer structure member that indicates the current file position, the one where the next character would normally be written. This is the variable that must be reset by vseek( ). First, a check is made to be certain that the mode argument is within the range of 0 to 1. If not, an illegal argument value has been provided with a −1 value is returned to the calling program.

If the value is within range, then the first else-if construct tests for a mode argument of zero. If this is the case, then ptr->>vfiloc is set to the value of off. This automatically provides an offset from the beginning of the file, position 0. If the value of the mode argument is 1, the second else-if test detects this. Such a mode indicates that the offset is to be from the current file position, which is also the current value of ptr-.viloc. Therefore, the value of off must be added to the current location value. Mathematical shorthand is used here in:

ptr −>vfiloc + = off

which is an abbreviated way of writing:

ptr −>vfiloc = ptr −>vfiloc + off

in C language. This notation adds the offset value contained in off to the current value of ptr-vfiloc.

This is a very simple function that is used to reset the location of the file pointer to access the various elements of the memory file.

vclose( )

The vclose( ) function is provided to maintain conventional points of reference while maintaining a memory file. This function simply "clears" the memory file pointer, freeing it for use as a pointer to another file. This is done by assigning the first character in *ptr a value of NULL. No actual closing operation takes place because the memory file will be contained in memory as long as the computer remains activated, or until the memory file is erased with the vlink( ) function. The source code for vclose( ) follows:

```
vclose(ptr)
VFILE *ptr;
{
        *ptr = '\0';

}
```

Remember, all vclose( ) does is to assign a NULL value to structure's the memory file pointer. It is not mandatory that a memory file pointer be cleared before using the pointer for another file. The vopen( ) function could be used with the currently open file pointer to open another file. In this case, the original memory file name would be overwritten by the new. Again, vclose( ) is provided simply as a conventional tool when working with memory files. It exists to allow the programmer to use standard conventions to open, close, and to manipulate memory files.

vputc( )

For writing single characters to a file, C language has the putc( ) function which accepts two arguments. The first is the character to be written, and the second is the file pointer. The memory file equivalent is called vputc( ) and its source code is displayed below:

```
vputc(a, ptr)
int a;
VFILE *ptr;
{
     *(ptr->fiptr + ptr->vfiloc) = a;
     ++ptr->vfiloc;
}
```

The source code for this function is very similar to that used for vputs( ) described earlier in this chapter. However, vputs( ) is used to write a string of characters to a memory file, and vputc( ) is used to write only a single character per call. Therefore, vputc( ) simply assigns the single character value to the memory offset identified by the value of vfiloc. When the character has been written into memory, the value of vfiloc is incremented by one. In the vputs( ) function, this same operation took place; however, a while loop was used to continually write successive characters from the string argument, and to increment vfiloc with each character write.

vgetc( )

The complement of vputc( ) is the vgetc( ) function which retrieves a single character from a memory file. This latter function is the equivalent of the standard C function, fgetc( ) is shown in FIG. 5-4.

Whereas, vputc( ) wrote a single character to a byte in memory, vgetc( ) writes a single byte from memory to an integer variable and returns this

Fig. 5-4. vgetc ( ) retrieves a single character from a memory file.

```
vgetc(ptr)
VFILE *ptr;
{
        int a;

        a = *(ptr->fiptr + ptr->vfiloc);

        ++ptr->vfiloc;

        if (a == '\0')
                return(-1);
        else
                return(a);

}
```

value to the calling program. As soon as the byte is assigned, the value of vfiloc is incremented by one, thus advancing the memory file pointer to the next, sequential element or byte. The last two functions have written or retrieved file characters as integers. Remember that C language handles single characters as integers with values of from 0 to 255, each representing a character in the ASCII character set.

vlink( )

In C language disk filekeeping operations, the unlink( ) function is used to erase a file from the disk. The memory file functions reserve portions of the computer's RAM to write file-like information. These portions of memory are reserved and can be accessed only through the memory file pointer created by calling vopen( ). Once a memory file has been completely written, it is often copied to disk for more permanent storage. It may later be recalled and rewritten into a memory file during the course of execution of an expert systems program that needs access to the information.

Once the memory file has been saved to disk, or when it is no longer needed, it is desirous to clear the reserved block of memory used specifically for this memory file. To do this, the vlink( ) function is provided. This function does not actually erase information from memory, but it frees up the reserved block (puts it back in the free memory pool) so that it may be used by other functions that allocate memory. In fact, this is what the unlink( ) function does in C when called on to erase a disk file. The file is not really erased, but the area it consumes is opened to access by other file writing/saving functions.

Fig. 5-5. vlink ( ) clears a reserved block of memory.

```
vlink(a)
char *a;
{
      int i;

      for (i = 0; i <= fino; ++i)
          if (strcmp(a, finame[i]) == 0) {
              free(v[i]->fiptr);
              free(finame[i]);
              break;
          }

}
```

Eventually, the disk space it consumed is written over by another file. This is exactly what happens with vlink( ), except that memory space is made available to future writes instead of disk space. The source code for vlink( ) is shown in FIG. 5-5.

This function performs two basic operations. As is the case with unlink( ), vlink( ) accepts the name of the memory file as its only argument. Again, it must have the name of the memory file and not the file pointer! It then searches the list of all existing memory files for the name provided as its argument. External variable fino keeps track of the number of memory files in existence, and *finame[ ] contains their names. When the name is identified, v[ ]->>fiptr, the pointer to the structure that was accessed by the filename (and thus to the allocated memory), is freed using the standard C language free( ) function. Secondly, the memory reserved to hold the name in *finame[ ] is also freed using the same function. For all intents and purposes, the memory file is now erased and no longer exists or, more appropriately, is not accessible by conventional means.

SUMMARY

This discussion has shown that it is a fairly simple matter to write a basic set of functions which will allow very fast access to vast amounts of data by loading all data into RAM and accessing it directly. Additionally, the functions discussed closely mirror the C language standard filekeeping function set. This allows the memory file functions to be used in a familiar manner—just as though you were addressing disk files.

As was discussed at the beginning of this chapter, a conventional ramdisk may be used to accomplish the same purposes. In such instances, the standard filekeeping functions common to C language may be used. For all intents and purposes, the executing program will be convinced that it is writing to and reading from a disk file, even though all such access is redirected to RAM. However, the portability of such a program will be limited, and available free RAM will play a large determining factor in how applicable such a program is to a particular machine configuration.

Using the functions and routines outlined in this chapter, a higher degree of control and thus portability are maintained. There are still restrictions on the amount of memory required for executing a given program, but the programmer can directly control this factor by specifying the size of a memory file. In a ramdisk configuration, files may technically be of infinite size, and writes will continue until the operating system signals an out-of-memory condition.

The functions discussed in this chapter have served the author well in handling some fairly complex problems. These problems involved writing commercial software that addresses the difficulty associated with the accessing of large amounts of data in the quickest possible times. For expert systems, intelligent data bases, and general AI applications in C language, these functions should prove highly useful.

6
Expert Systems

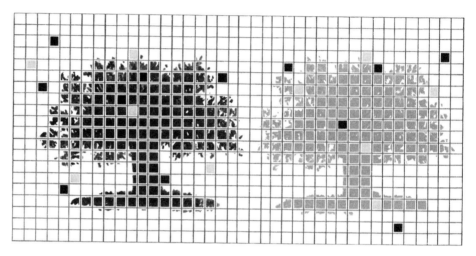

As is the case with the definition of artificial intelligence, there are many definitions for the term expert system. Generally speaking, you can think of knowledge-based expert systems as computer hardware/software that uses knowledge and inference procedures to solve problems that are so complex that they normally require the intervention of human beings with expertise in the problem area.

Too many people outside the AI field tend to think of expert systems as those intelligent computers that many of us were subjected to in science fiction magazines. If you will recall, such computers were far smarter than any human being (supposedly because they contain the complete knowledge of the entire human race). Many of them even took control and ended up being rulers of the entire human race until some janitor accidentally pulled out the power plug while cleaning behind the hundreds of tons of equipment that made up the device.

Artificial intelligence has progressed far in the relatively short time it has been a subject of human study. However, we are still more than a few years away from building a computer that is capable of ruling the human race.

Such a device as I've described here was all knowing, all seeing, and all powerful. What has been discussed here is not really artificial intelligence, but artificial super-intelligence: intelligence far beyond that of any single human being.

I will move away from this futuristic phantasm and come down to Earth again, so I can pragmatically discuss expert systems. What do you think of when the word expert is mentioned? Perhaps you think of a nuclear scientist, but you may also think of your neighborhood plumber. After all, the plumber is an expert when it comes to plumbing. Your plumber may not be able to quote Shakespeare or perform quantum mechanics, but that nuclear scientist may not be expert enough to fix a cracked pipe either.

For the discussions in this book, an expert will be defined as someone, or even some device, that has more than common knowledge within a specific area. For instance, you may know how to replace the washer in a faucet in order to get rid of a persistent leak. We might say that everyone may not know how to do this, but many people do. Therefore, you would not be considered an expert in the plumbing field because of your knowledge limitations. You're not totally ignorant when it comes to plumbing, but you're not an expert either.

On the other hand, if you knew how to solder pipes, install drain fields, construct new plumbing lines, etc., then you would possess more than the "average" amount of knowledge within the plumbing field. You may not be a plumber, but you may possess the knowledge needed to be one. This, then, would label you an expert.

But an expert at what? The answer to this, obviously, is plumbing. Your demonstrated knowledge is sufficient to allow you to claim expertise in this area because your total knowledge concept of plumbing is more than that of the average individual. For the purpose of this discussion, I will not define an average individual because that could take the next 300 pages. Suffice it to say that the average person does not possess an expert level of plumbing knowledge.

Now, as an expert plumber, does this mean that you are automatically an expert in any other area? The answer is no. You may be, but this cannot be ascertained by simply asking you questions that test your knowledge of plumbing. For the most part, human beings might be adept at many different pursuits, but are experts in only one or two. Therefore, to think that an artificially intelligent machine would be expert in many, many subjects would be to expect the machine to be far smarter than any human being instead of just as smart as one.

In artificial intelligence programming, the idea is to develop certain algorithms, programs, and systems that either mimic some of the attributes of human thinking or can at least provide information that is similar to the information an expert human would provide.

How is this done?

The first objective from the programming side involves the building of a vehicle: a program that can access a large amount of data, and process this data based upon several moderately complex rules. Some of these rules have been discussed in previous chapters. The large database would contain the identified knowledge of an also identified human expert in a particular field. In the human being supplying knowledge to that database is an expert in plumbing, then the proper manipulation of this data by the vehicle might yield a system that is also expert in the plumbing field. If the human being supplying knowledge to the database is a fishing expert, then you might arrive at an expert system for fishing.

To go one step further, by combining both databases and using the same vehicle, an expert system could be built with twofold expertise: first, in the area of plumbing, and then in the area of fishing.

However, how is this data sampled? How do you know what questions to ask? Questions must be asked in order for the expert system to gain data from which an assumption can be made, and information transferred.

THE EXPERT PLUMBER

Let's examine this concept more thoroughly by going through the motions of what occurs when the plumber comes to your house. First of all, plumbers must know why they were called. You just don't call the plumber and say "I have a plumbing problem. Send me a plumber."

Right away, the person on the other end of that phone will probably ask "What seems to be the problem?"

Again, you are not the plumbing expert, but you experienced something that prompted you to think you need a plumber. The expert on the other end of the phone is simply pumping you for more information—information that only an eyewitness can supply. The expert on the phone does not initially provide expert advice. Rather, expert questions are asked that are designed to elicit useful data from a non-expert.

Perhaps the expert plumber can determine by phone what the problem is. Such a diagnosis is based upon incomplete data, but that plumber may be expert enough, and may remember enough life experiences, to have calculated the probability of the problem to a very high degree. This is the inference part of the two-way conversation.

This scenario has taken the following route:

1) Expert is consulted by non-expert.
2) Expert asks non-expert reason for consultation.
3) Expert questions are asked of the non-expert.
4) Expert receives data from non-expert based upon answers.
5) Expert infers course of action from attained data.

With this knowledge, the plumber can calculate with reasonable accuracy what is needed to effect a repair and plan to do the job.

Now, let's assume that you consulted the plumber because you noticed that your sink was not draining properly. During the phone conversation, the plumber asks you if the sink was draining all right yesterday and if any other sinks in the home are similarly affected. Your response is that the problem just started today and, upon checking, every sink in the home is not draining properly.

From this bit of information, the plumber has learned that the drain problem is a central problem and not confined to any one drain. Therefore, the indication is that the blockage must be at some central point in the home, possibly near the point where the plumbing from all drains converges and travels out to the street mains.

Now, the plumber may want to ask you additional questions that may require your traveling down to the basement to see if there is a major trap at any point just prior to the house lines entering the main sewer system. Based upon your answer, the plumber may ask you to perform other checks. The entire procedure is a system of asking the right question and obtaining an informative, if not expert, answer. To be a little more explicit, the expert is able to condense the need for complex data into a simple question that will allow that data to be given by a non-expert. The real trick to deciphering the problem is knowing which questions to ask and the proper way to ask them.

I'll carry this scenario one step further and assume that the plumber cannot actually come by the home and correct the problem, but is trying to talk you through the process of effecting a repair on your own. Based upon your answers to the plumber's expert questions, you may be advised to remove the cap on the last trap in the line and remove any debris from that trap. I will assume that this advice is indeed accurate and that the repair is effected.

To make this discussion even more interesting, assume that the plumber was actually in his truck at the time of your call, and his secretary relayed his questions via two-way radio to you and your answers to him.

With this in mind, you will now consult an expert system on plumbing with the same problem. You bring up the system, and the first question asked is "What seems to be the problem?"

Your response is "My sink is stopped up."

The next question displayed on the screen by the expert system is "Is this problem localized to the sink in question, or does it occur in every sink in the home?"

Your response is "All sinks are stopped up."

The next question from the expert system is "Is there a trap just prior to your plumbing entering the outside line?"

Your response is "Yes."

The expert system pauses to make inferences from the supplied data. Its next response is "Remove the cap from the trap and clean out all debris."

The expert/non-expert relationship discussed here is nearly identical to the one discussed previously, which involved a human plumber. Both the plumber and the expert system arrived at the same conclusion based upon the same input of data. In this example, it would make no difference whether you consulted the expert plumber or the expert system.

Because I'm dealing with "what ifs" here, maybe it is just possible that the secretary at the plumber's office really isn't talking to the plumber on the two-way radio, but instead actually consulting an expert system in the office computer. Maybe the plumber died a year ago, and this is the only way they could stay in business. In any event, the correct questions were asked and the same diagnosis was reached.

The expert system can take the place of a human being who is also expert in the same field, but that system cannot exist, cannot even be initially built, without the direct input from the human expert. In building expert systems, we must identify the problems that can occur so that the right questions may be asked. You will notice that in both of the above scenarios, the person who initially consulted the expert really didn't ask any questions. The expert, be it human or machine, asked the questions once the caller supplied the initial problem.

The prime operation of an expert system depends upon the system getting input data to compare with expert information that is already contained in its database. Once enough data has been input, enough comparisons can be made to arrive at an intelligent inference. When you get right down to it, the expert system operates in a similar manner to a troubleshooting manual that might be supplied with a piece of electronic equipment. Such manuals are designed for the consumer and generally list an occurrence such as "Light won't come on," a possible cause such as "Fuse blown," and the problem corrective procedure, "Replace fuse."

This same line of exploration is what we try to effect, but on a more involved and complex level via the expert system.

In building an expert system, the first thing that must be decided is in what area or areas will this system be expert? The second factor to consider is where is this expert information going to come from in order that the proper database may be constructed. The third and final criteria is that of the vehicle that will be used to accept user input, compare it with information in the database, and make proper inferences from the comparisons.

"IS IT A MAMMAL?"

Begin with an expert system that will be expert in one very narrow area of biology. This expert system will determine whether or not an animal that the user has in mind is a mammal or some other type of animal or object. The program follows:

```
main()
{
    int x;

    puts("Does this animal nurse its young(Y/N)?");
    scanf("%d", &x);

    if (x == 'Y')
        puts("The animal is a mammal.");
    else
        puts("The animal is not a mammal.");
}
```

This is a bonafide expert system. It never makes a mistake as long as the user provides the correct input. Its area of expertise is in knowing whether something is a mammal by asking a single question. If the answer to the question is yes, the animal is a mammal. If the answer is negative, the animal is not a mammal.

"Ridiculous!" you might exclaim. However, this is pretty much the way all expert systems start out. This simple expert system will be examined in reference to the construction steps mentioned earlier. First of all, determine in what area our expert system is to be expert. This system is expert in determining whether an animal is a mammal. Secondly, decide from where the expert information to form our database is to come. In this instance, the information comes from our expert, which happens to be Webster's New Collegiate Dictionary, which defines a mammal as "any of a class of higher vertebrates comprising man and all other animals that nurse their young with milk secreted by mammary glands and have skin usually more or less covered with hair." All mammals have one thing in common: they nurse their young with milk. No other animals nurse their young with milk; therefore, if an animal nurses its young with milk, it is a mammal.

The third part of the expert system is the vehicle or processing section that manipulates and compares data. In this program, the vehicle is the if statement that performs a conditional test. In this example, the database consists of only one element, and this element is found in the single question that is asked: "Does this animal nurse its young?" This is the expert question that is asked of the non-expert user. The scanf( ) statement retrieves the user input from the keyboard. If the response is 'Y' then the conditional test determines that the "it is a mammal" result is displayed. Still in the conditional test, the else portion of the statement takes over if the user input is other than 'Y'. In this case, the "is not a mammal" result is displayed.

There you have it: your first expert system, and with almost no pain or bother. However, a previous discussion stated that an expert system possessed more knowledge about a certain subject than the average individual. This particular program does not meet that criteria exactly, but I will assume that any person who would need to use this program is far less expert on the subject of mammals than the program is—so such a person would have no need of it.

On a more serious note, this simple example will serve as a very elementary starting point from which a fairly respectable expert system can be built.

Again, a major role of an expert system is to ask the proper questions. To do this, the builder of the system must have some general idea of the type of persons who will be using the system. A previous example of an expert system that addressed plumbing can be considered an expert system only if you don't make a living as a plumber. However, suppose you wanted to build an expert system that could be used by plumbers to diagnose more difficult problems. The initial expert system was designed to be accessed by persons who were not plumbers. Therefore, it is written so that it will ask questions appropriate to a non-expert user level. This new concept would ask questions applicable to persons who are expert plumbers, and who need an even more expert opinion. Needless to say, both systems would contain different questions and respond in different ways to the answers that were received.

With this in mind, continue with our mammal-detecting example and assume that the user does not know what a mammal is, but can describe certain attributes of the animal based upon the questions asked by the expert system. To make the example as simple as possible, make sure all answers can be responded to with a yes or no equivalent. In fact, this is the way most expert systems operate.

An expert system normally has to ask many questions in order to arrive at an output. Assume that the user of our mammal-identifying expert system may not know all of the answers that the system might ask. This means that you can build in a routine that will react to such an event and try to arrive at the correct answer anyway by asking still other questions.

In FIG. 6-1, the else-if statement takes into account a third possible answer by the user—one that indicates the user does not know the correct answer to a question the expert has asked. When this is the case, the else portion of this predicate controls another routine that asks another question. In this example, the answer to this question can only be yes or no. Another else statement sequence is entered that evaluates the results of the answer to this second question. Notice that the word "probably" has been inserted into the response lines within this portion of the program. This reflects the expert system's doubts about the ability of the user to correctly answer simple questions. In other words, if the first question could not be answered, perhaps the second question wasn't answered accurately either. The expert hedges a bit by stating that

Fig. 6-1. This program allows for a "don't know" answer.

```
/* D = Don't Know */
main()
{
    int x;

    puts("Does this animal nurse its young(Y/N/D)?");
    scanf("%d", &x);

    if (x == 'Y')
        puts("This animal is a mammal");
    else if (x == 'N')
        puts("This animal is not a mammal");
    else {
        puts("Is this a furry, warm-blooded animal(Y/N)?");
        scanf("%d", &x);
        if (x == 'Y')
            puts("This animal is probably a mammal");
        if (x == 'N')
            puts("This animal is probably not a mammal");
    }
}
```

available information would indicate that the animal in question is, more than likely, a mammal.

Pursuing the multiple question expert system idea a bit further: it can be stated that the certainty of an outcome becomes more assured when more and more data has been obtained. A value can be put on different types of data that are derived from various questions. In the case of the mammal, it can be stated that if the animal in question nurses its young then it is 100% certain that it is a mammal. Likewise, if it does not nurse its young, then it is a 100% certainty that it is not a mammal. Working on a scale of 0 to 1 (0 = no mammal and 1 = mammal), we can give ratings to the answers to various questions. When the rating becomes or exceeds, then the expert can output its answer with far more certainty. Also, if the expert should run out of questions and still not have arrived at 1, then a best guess can be made based upon whether the added rating values are above or below 0.50.

A program that will perform these described operations is shown in FIG. 6-2. This program is quite simple, but it allows us to explore a little deeper into the field of expert systems written in C language.

Integer variables x and ct are used to hold retrieved information from the keyboard and to access preprogrammed questions respectively. Double precision variable y is used to hold the changing value that indicates whether enough evidence has been obtained to declare the animal or mammal or not. The array of char pointers q is used to point to the memory location of five different questions that must be answered by the user.

The last variable is declared a static double two dimensional array that forms a 5×2 matrix of values, which correspond to yes (Y) and no (N) responses to each of the five questions. For instance, if the answer to question number one is yes (Y) then the value at array position, 0,0 will be assigned to a variable. If the answer to the same question is no (N), then the value at array position 0,1 is assigned to the variable.

Again, each of these values corresponds directly to an equivalent question which is accessed by the array of pointers. The statement char *q[ ] contains 5 pointers of type char. Each of these is made to point to a single text string which is contained within double quotation marks in the assignment lines that follow. Remember, a pointer is a special variable that is used to point to a specific memory location. It cannot "hold" any value (other than this memory address) as is the case with standard variables. Via the five assignment lines, each of the five pointers in this array are made to point to the memory locations where these questions are written.

Fig. 6-2. This program performs a best guess.

```c
main()
{
    int x, ct;
    double y;
    char *q[5];

    static double z[5][2] = {
         { 0.33, -1.0 },
         { -0.75, 0.25 },
         { -0.75, 0.25 },
         { 0.75, -0.75 },
         { 1.0, -1.0 }
    };

    q[0] = "Does this animal have bones(Y/N/D)?";
    q[1] = "Does this animal fly(Y/N/D)?";
    q[2] = "Does this animal have a bill(Y/N/D)?";
    q[3] = "Does this animal have fur(Y/N/D)?";
    q[4] = "Does this animal nurse its young(Y/N/D)?";

    x = ct = 0;
    y = 0.0;

    printf("EXPERT SYSTEM\n\n");
    printf("   MAMMALS\n\n");

    while (y > -1 && y < 1 && ct < 5) {
        printf("%s\n", q[ct]);
        x = toupper(getch());
        if (x == 'Y')
            x = 0;
        else if (x == 'N')
            x = 1;
        else {
            ++ct;
            continue;
        }
        y += z[ct++][x];

    }

    if (y >= 1.0)
        printf("This animal is a mammal\n");
    else if (y <= -1)
        printf("This animal is not a mammal\n");
    else if (y > 0)
        printf("This animal is probably a mammal\n");
    else if (y < 0)
        printf("This animal is probably not a mammal\n");
    else
        printf("Not enough information to decide\n");

}
```

The first question is "Does this animal have bones (Y/N/D)?" A **Y** means yes, the **N** means no, and the **D** means don't know. Again, these answers to this first question are given numeric values that are contained in positions 0,0 and 0,1 of the static double array named by the letter z. If the answer to this question is yes, then a value of 0.33 is accessed within the array. Assuming that −1 equates to "Not a mammal" and +1 equates to "Is a mammal" then it can be said that the value of 0.33 would indicate that, if the animal in question has bones, then there is a 33 percent chance that it will be a mammal. On the other hand, if the answer to question number one is no, then a value of −1 is accessed within the array matrix. This means that the animal is definitely not a mammal because it contains no bones. No further questions need be asked.

This sequence of asking questions and assigning numeric values based upon a yes or no response continues for the next four questions, assuming that a value of −1 or +1 is not reached when the results of each question are added to the results from the previous question. A response of "Don't Know" results in a value of zero.

All of the above procedures are carried out from within the confines of a while( ) loop. Before entering this loop, the matrix is loaded and the pointer array is assigned. Also, variables x, y, and ct are initialized to zero. Double precision variable y keeps track of the math after each question is answered. When y is equal to −1 or to +1, the loop is exited due to the control clause used when the loop is established. From this point on, the value in y is passed through an else-if construct to determine what response to write to the screen.

Upon entering the while( ) loop, the first question, pointed to by q[ct], is displayed using the printf( ) function. At this pint, ct is equal to a value of zero which was assigned prior to loop entry. Next, the getch( ) function is used in conjunction with the toupper( )function to get the user's single key input. The toupper function automatically converts any lower case character to upper case which makes determination a lot easier for routines to follow. An if-else construct is now entered that determines the value in x and reassigns this same variable a numerical value of 0, or 1, corresponding to 'Y' or 'N'. If x should be equal to 'D', the else portion of this predicate simply increments ct by one and uses the continue statement to cause the next loop cycle to take place. However, if the response to the question was either 'Y' or 'N', then the value in x is used to access the proper value found in the static double array z. A 'Y' causes variable y to be assigned its current value (zero at this point) plus the value in 0,0 or 0.33. The assignment line:

y += z[ct++][x]

on the first pass of the loop (and assuming a 'Y' answer to the first question) breaks down to:

y = y + z[0][0]

If the first question was responded to with a 'N', then the result would be to access the second array element as in:

y = y + z[0][1]

In this latter case, y would be equal to −1.0. Notice that ct is incremented within the assignment line with the incremental operator (++). Because the operator follows the variable, the initial value of ct (which is zero at this point) is used before the variable is incremented to +1.

The loop cycles again. If the first question received a positive answer, then the next question is displayed and the procedure starts all over again with the value of y being added to or subtracted from. However, if the first question received a negative reply, then y is equal to −1 and the escape clause of the loop is met (i.e. y is no longer more than −1) and the loop terminates.

Assume that the first question was answered (Y). This means that y is now equal to 0.33. Assume, also, that the animal is a bear. The next question would be displayed, which asks if the animal flies. The answer to this would be 'N' so y would be incremented by itself plus 0.25. This value is found at position 1,1 in the array matrix. This position is accessed because ct is now equal to 1 and the 'N' response caused x to be assigned a value of 1. Therefore:

z[ct][x] = z[1][1] = 0.25

Now, y is incremented by 0.25 for a value of 0.58. We are now better than 50% sure that the animal is a mammal, but the questions will continue until the expert is 100% sure, or there are no more questions to ask. The next loop cycle asks if the animal has a bill. The answer is 'N', so the sixth value in the array is accessed which adds another 0.25 to the current value of y. This variable is now equal to 0.83. The expert is now very sure that the animal is a mammal, but it is still not certain. The next question asks if the animal has fur. The answer to this is 'Y' which accesses a value of 0.75 from the array. Variable y is now equal to 1.58. The expert now knows with certainty that the animal is a mammal. When the loop tries to go around one more time, the escape test reveals that variable y is no longer equal to a value of less that +1. The loop terminates and the value in y is read by the if-else construct.

The if-else test is quite simple and closely resembles the one used in a previous program. Simply put, if y is more than or equal to 1, then the "Is a mammal" phrase is written to the screen. If y is less than or equal to −1, then the "Is not a mammal" phrase is written. However, it is also possible (due to the user not knowing the answer to some questions and responding with a 'D') that y will still be of a fractional value of more than −1 and less than +1. Here, the if-else construct makes a best guess. If the value is more than zero then the "Probably is a mammal" phrase is written. If the value in y is less than zero, then the "Probably is not a mammal" phrase comes up.

It is also possible that y could be equal to zero. In this case, the expert hedges and prints a phrase telling the user that it doesn't have enough information to infer a reasonable answer.

While this might be termed an "Expert System" it is not really a practical system for broad-ranging applications. This is certainly a dedicated program that requires every possible question and resulting answer to be programmed into its source code. Obviously, many other types of applications could be tackled in an elementary fashion by this program through a prudent change in source code questions and results. Equally obvious is the fact that the numeric quantities allotted to each "YES/NO" answer are crucial to the reliability of the conclusions this program eventually outputs to the user.

So, in the elementary Expert System just discussed, the programmer must decide the questions, the resulting answers and the "rule" by which these answers are arrived at. The programmer must decide the value of a yes or no answer and, in short, must decide every aspect of the program. This method is quite limiting and certainly is not suitable to any practical Expert System applications. The program, however, does make an excellent first example in the study of artificial intelligence as it relates to expert systems in general.

Before straying too far from this elementary example, it should be understood that expert systems must necessarily be designed to anticipate any question that might be asked about the subject area that system is expert in. However, this does not mean that each and every question must be a part of the program source code. Likewise, the answer to each and every question does not need to be a part of this source code.

This last series of statements may sound very confusing, but this can be easily cleared up. If all questions and answers must be anticipated by the expert system, then it would stand to reason that all questions and answers must be a part of the program source code that makes up that expert system. Wrong! All the programmer needs to do is build in the routines that will allow for expert "users" to supply the questions and the answers. In other words, the expert system is nothing more than a vehicle for questions, values and answers supplied by persons who may be true experts in a certain field, but who know little or nothing about computer programming. There are many parallel examples of this. In fact almost every piece of business or corporate software falls into the "vehicle" category though not necessarily in the field of artificial intelligence.

Take for instance the various data base programs available. None of these contain data base information. Each contains the vehicle for loading in the information that will make up the data base. The other aspect of this "vehicle" is the means to manipulate, process and recall the information. Again, the information that goes into the data base is user supplied. The vehicle for allowing this information to be input, stored, processed, manipulated, and recalled is the programmer's responsibility.

TOWARD A GENERIC EXPERT

The program in FIG. 6-3 is similar to the first regarding output information. However, it appears to be (and indeed is) more complex. The complexities involved relate to the program's capability of accepting and storing user-input questions and results. This means that the data base contained within this expert system is variable and may address any topic any user may desire, providing that the expert information can be properly loaded.

A certain amount of filekeeping is involved in this program. This is absolutely mandatory if the program is to be used for worthwhile purposes as opposed to simply serving as an example. The expert information that is input along with the results is stored on disk, and may be reloaded after the computer has been shut down and then brought back on line.

Again, the program may look complex, especially when compared with the one discussed previously, but by taking the program in blocks, you should have little difficulty acquiring a full understanding. Just remember that much of this program's complexity involves reading and writing file information.

To gain a full understanding of the program in FIG. 6-3, be sure to remember that it works in the same manner as the previous one. In this program, however, it is up to the human expert to supply the questions, the value a yes or no answer receives, and the results. Once the human expert has transferred their knowledge to this expert system, less knowledgeable persons may use it effectively.

Fig. 6-3. This program has a variable database.

```c
main()
{
int x, ct;
double y, z[100][2];
char q[5][100], ques[80], num1[10], num2[10];
char res[20][100];
FILE *fp, *fpp;

ct = 1;

printf("Do you wish to construct a data bank(Y/N)\n");
if ((x = toupper(getch())) == 'Y') {
    if ((fp = fopen("xpbase", "w")) == NULL) {
        printf("Can't open data base file%d\n", 7);
        exit(0);
    }
    while(x) {
        printf("Type question #%d\n", ct++);
        gets(ques);
        if (strcmp(ques, "end") == 0) {
            fclose(fp);
            break;
        }
        printf("If answered yes, what is the value?\n");
        gets(num1);
        printf("If answered no, what is the value?\n");
        gets(num2);

        fprintf(fp, "%s:%s:\n%s\n", num1, num2, ques);

    }
    fclose(fp);

    ct = 0;

    if ((fpp = fopen("xpresult", "w")) == NULL) {
        printf("Can't open result file.\n");
        exit(0);
    }

    printf("Type the result of a positive outcome\n");
    gets(res[ct]);
    fprintf(fpp, "%s\n", res[ct++]);
    printf("\n\nType the result of a negative outcome.\n");
    gets(res[ct]);
    fprintf(fpp, "%s\n", res[ct++]);
    printf("\n\nType the result of a probable positive outcome.\n");
    gets(res[ct]);
    fprintf(fpp, "%s\n", res[ct++]);
    printf("\n\nType the result of a probable negative outcome.\n");
    gets(res[ct]);
    fprintf(fpp, "%s\n", res[ct]);
```

(Fig. 6-3 cont.)

```
        fclose(fpp);
    }
    printf("Do you wish to use the Expert System(Y/N)?");
    x = toupper(getch());

    if (x == 'N') {
        printf("\n\nExpert System Data Base is loaded\n");
        exit(0);
    }

    if ((fp = fopen("xpbase", "r")) == NULL) {
        printf("Data Base Unavailable\n");
        exit(0);
    }

    if ((fpp = fopen("xpresult", "r")) == NULL) {
        printf("Data Base Results Unavailable\n");
        exit(0);
    }

    x = y = ct = 0;

    while (fgets(ques, 200, fp) != NULL) {
        sscanf(ques, "%lf:%lf:", &z[ct][0], &z[ct][1]);
        fgets(q[ct++], 200, fp);
    }

    ct = 0;

    while (fgets(res[ct++], 99, fpp) != NULL)
        ;

    fclose(fp);
    fclose(fpp);

    printf("\n\nData base has been loaded into memory\n");

    x = y = ct = 0;

    printf("EXPERT SYSTEM\n\n");
    printf("    MAMMALS\n\n");

    while (y > -1 && y < 1 && ct < 5) {
        printf("%s\n", q[ct]);
        x = toupper(getch());
        if (x == 'Y')
            x = 0;
        else if (x == 'N')
            x = 1;
        else {
            ++ct;
            continue;
        }
```

(Fig. 6-3 cont.)

```
            y += z[ct++][x];
    }
    if (y >= 1.0)
        puts(res[0]);
    else if (y <= -1.0)
        puts(res[1]);
    else if (y > 0)
        puts(res[2]);
    else if (y < 0)

        puts(res[3]);
        else
            printf("Not enough information to decide\n");

}
```

After the variables have been declared, a printf function is used to display the opening prompt, which asks the user whether they wish to construct a data bank. This would be the thing to do upon first invoking the program, and before any data has been loaded to disk. This option would also be chosen if the current data bank were to be purged, and a new one loaded. Assume for now that this is the first run of the program and the expert system is completely ignorant. It has no data bank, does not know what questions to ask, and has no idea of results.

The if statement line that follows the printf function tests for keyboard input. This construct may seem unusual to beginning C language programmers. This line tests for an input of 'Y' or 'N'. To make things as convenient as possible, the getch() function is used, which will trap for a single key press. Remember, the purpose of an expert system is to aid people who are not expert in the subject area and may have even less expertise at working with computers.

Because it is possible that the keyboard could be in upper or lowercase mode, the toupper function is used with getch() as its argument. The toupper() function assures that the final return to variable x within the if statement line will always be uppercase. Assuming that the keyboard is in lower case mode, getch() would return a lowercase 'y' (for instance). The toupper function would automatically convert this to uppercase 'Y', which would be assigned to variable x. If the keyboard were in uppercase mode, then toupper would not modify the return from getch(). This type of operation is simple and provides a slightly higher degree of user friendliness.

Assuming that the response is 'Y,' a data base file is opened in the name of "xpbase"—an arbitrary name. The fopen( ) function is used from within the safe confines of an if statement line. The if statement checks for a return of NULL from fopen( ). This is always a necessity when opening a file because, if the file cannot be opened for some reason, a very difficult debugging procedure might ensue—assuming that your system did not provide a prompt. In this instance, if the file cannot be opened for any reason, fopen( ) will return NULL. The if statement looks for this occurrence and displays a prompt, then terminates the program should a NULL occur.

Assuming that the file is successfully opened in write ("w") mode, a while loop is entered that prompts the expert for input. Another printf function is used to prompt the expert to input sequentially numbered questions. The numbering sequence is counted by variable ct. This variable is used as the integer argument to the printf function and is then incremented by 1 on each pass of the while loop. After each prompt, the gets( ) function retrieves the keyboard input, writing it to char array ques. This loop is exited when ques contains "end". This is tested for by the if statement line that follows gets( ). In this line, the strcmp( ) function compares the content of ques with "end". If the human expert has input "end" then the xpbase file is closed and the loop is exited via the break statement.

After each question is input, a prompt is written to the screen that asks for the value of a yes answer, and the value of a no answer. These values will be positive for a positive reply, and negative for a negative reply. They will span the distance between 0 and plus or minus 1. Each response by the human expert is captured by the gets( ) function. In other words, the numeric value input for each answer is actually input as a character string.

The final program statement within the loop is fprintf( ). This function writes formatted output to a designated file. The control statement in this function is:

"%s:%s:\n%s\n"

The arguments to fprintf( ) are num1, num2, ques. The first two represent the values for yes and no answers to each question. The last variable contains the text of the question. Assuming that num1 and num2 are equal to 0.5, respectively, and that ques is equal to "Does this animal nurse its young (Y/N/D)?", then the following single line will be written to the file:

0.5:-0.5:newline characters
Does this animal nurse its young (Y/N/D)? newline character

This sequence will continue for each question. The positive and negative values for that question will be written on one file line, followed by a newline character. The question for which these values pertain will be written to the next line, and subsequently followed by a newline character.

When the human expert types "end" the loop is exited and the file is closed by means of the fclose( ) function.

Now, this doesn't seem to be such a complex operation at all, but in expert system and artificial intelligence terminology, this program has accomplished something. It has learned! The information that the human expert has is now placed within the data bank of the computer. This data bank not only contains the correct question to ask, but the value that should be placed on any one question. A bit later, I will discuss another aspect of this program that establishes the rules for judging all of the acquired data values. Additionally, the final results or expert answers will be decided based upon these judgment rules.

At this juncture in the program, the data base has been loaded. Perhaps it would be more accurate to state that a portion of the data base has been saved. We still have not arrived at the results based upon the values that are input by the non-expert user to the questions that will be asked. The next section of the program addresses the result portion of our miniature expert system.

A new file is opened in much the same manner as the first. This one is given the arbitrary name of "xpresult". Next, a series of prompts is written to the screen asking the human expert the result of various outcomes. As with the previous program example, the simplistic rule used for determining results is based on a final value that is positive or negative. Therefore, the first result prompt asks the human expert what result to display should the final numeric total be positive.

The gets( ) function retrieves the keyboard input and assigns it to char array res[ ]. Integer variable ct is initialized to zero prior to entering this program segment. Therefore, this first array position res[ct] is zero. Now, the fprintf( ) function is used to write the contents of this array position to the opened file. The argument to fprintf( ) is r[ct++], which actually does two things. First, the contents of r[ct] are returned to fprintf( ), but once the return has been effected, the value of ct is incremented by one. Therefore, when r[ct++] is first executed, ct is equal to zero. Immediately afterward, however, ct is equal to one.

The next prompt asks for the result of a negative outcome, with the ensuing call to gets( ) and fprintf( ). If you will recall from the previous program, a total value of +1 or !1 indicated definite positive or negative results, respectively. However, based upon the non-expert user's lack of knowledge, total values can sometimes be less than +1 but more than zero or less than zero but more than !1. Neither or these mathematical conditions indicates a definite positive or definite negative result. Therefore, it is necessary to develop rules that will obtain the best answer by inference. In this case, a value that is negative results in a "probable" negative outcome, whereas a value that is positive (but less than +1) results in a "probable" positive outcome. Prompts are written asking the human expert to input the results for these probable outcomes.

Following these operations, the complete data base has been loaded into two disk files named "xpbase" and "xpresult" respectively. The "tutoring" aspect of making this program "intelligent" is now complete. The only thing left to do is to exercise the remainder of the program to see how effective this educational experience has been.

At this juncture, a non-expert user is asked if they wish to use the expert system. This same prompt would appear if you had shut down the system after the database was loaded and then brought the program back up again following an 'N' response to the first prompt that asks if you want to construct a data bank.

The user response is handed to variable x and is retrieved via the getch( ) function. Again, the toupper( ) function is used to assure an upper case response. If the answer to this prompt is 'N' then a message is displayed stating that the data base is loaded and the program is terminated. If the response is 'Y' then xpbase is opened for read access, as is xpresult. All active variables are initialized to zero and a loop is entered.

In the "tutoring" process, values in char arrays were read into the files. Here, the opposite takes place as file values are read into the char arrays. Within the while loop, fgets( ) reads a single line into char array ques. Then, the sscanf( ) function is used to read information from ques into, first, the double precision numeric array z. Next, fgets( ) is used again to read the next line from the file directly into char array (two-dimensional) q.

The sscanf( ) function is normally put to little use, especially by beginning programmers. This function works in the same manner as scanf( ) and fscanf( ). However, whereas these last two functions read formatted input from the keyboard and from disk files, respectively, sscanf( ) reads formatted input from a char array, allowing it to be written to memory locations specified by its control string and by its pointer arguments. This use of sscanf( ) simply converts the two numeric values contained in ques to double-precision, floating-point numbers that are written at the memory locations pointed to by the addresses of the array variables. Notice that the ampersand (&) precedes each of the array arguments. This means that the arguments are pointers and name the memory locations set aside for storage to these array positions.

This usage closely mimics atof( ), a function used to pull a numeric quantity (double precision) from a string argument. For the sake of convenience and for storage efficiency, the values that obtain for yes and no answers to a specific question are written to the same file line. The fgets( ) function retrieves them as a single text unit. However, sscanf( ) is able to retrieve each of the two numeric values and write them as numbers to the proper variable, because the format of the text argument is known ahead of time. The colon separators are not mandatory, but were written to the file as an easy means of identifying separate values.

When the colon is encountered by sscanf( ), all scanning for that particular field ceases. However, if a space or any other non-numeric character was likewise encountered, the same cessation of scanning would occur.

The file reading operations described above apply only to xpbase, the file that contained the questions and their response values. File pointer *fp points to this open file. Another file was opened with a pointer named *fpp. This pointer accesses the xpresult file.

The next while loop also uses fgets( ) and reads the result information from xpresult directly into the res[ ] array. You will remember that an earlier operation read information out of this array into the file. This is the exact reverse of that operation.

When the loop is exited (upon end of file), two fclose( ) functions are used to close all file access. A message states that the data base has been loaded into memory, and you are finally ready to actually make use of your expert system.

Because this program came about as a result of our previous mammal identification program, we will assume that this expert system is also adept at identifying mammals, because a mammal expert (presumably) has input data about mammals to the data base. This is similar data to that which was used for our previous program. Therefore, shown here is the program run already discussed for loading expert data:

Do you wish to construct a data bank) (Y/N)? Y

Type question #1: Does this animal have bones (Y/N/D)?
If answered yes, what is the value? 0.33
If answered no, what is the value? 10.0

Type question #2: Does this animal fly (Y/N/D)?
If answered yes, what is the value? −0.75
If answered no, what is the value? 0.25

Type question #3: Does this animal have a bill (Y/N/D)?
If answered yes, what is the value? −0.75
If answered no, what is the value? 0.25

Type question #4: Does this animal have fur (Y/N/D)?
If answered yes, what is the value? 0.75
If answered no, what is the value? -0.75

Type question #5: Does this animal have its young (Y/N/D)?
If answered yes, what is the value? 10.0
If answered no, what is the value? -10.0

Type question #6: end (Signal to terminate question list)

Type the result of a positive outcome: Animal is a mammal.

Type the result of a negative outcome: Animal is not a mammal.

Type the result of a probable positive outcome:
Animal is probably a mammal.

Type the result of a probable negative outcome:
Animal is probably not a mammal.

This replay of the expert loading will help you to coordinate the following description of the actual expert system run.

Immediately after the EXPERT SYSTEM/MAMMALS prompt is displayed on the screen, a while loop is entered. It should be remembered that variable y contains the added results of each question. This particular program was set up as an example only and allows a maximum of five questions to be asked. This is true because char array q is dimensioned with only five subscripts, each of which may be 100 characters in length. However, if you wish to ask more questions, all that would be necessary would be to increase the subscript value.

In any event, the while loop tests for a condition of y being more than -1 and y being less than 1 and ct being less than 5. As long as this conglomerate condition is true, the loop will continue to cycle. However, should y reach a value of -1 or less or y reach a value of +1 or more or ct (the variable that keeps track of the number of questions) attain a value of 5, the loop will terminate. You will note from the discussion about the previous program that a condition of 1.0 or -1.0 indicates a definite result. Therefore, should the non-expert user's response to questions result in a value of -1.0 or +1.0 or a value that is more than the absolute value of either of these two quantities, a result may be arrived at without asking further questions. This brings about loop termination, as does answering the fifth and final question.

On each pass of the loop, a printf( ) function is used to display the question, which is responded to with 'Y', 'N', or 'D'. Actually, the if statement lines only test for occurrence of the first two characters. Any other character equates to a 'D' for "don't know."

You will again see the familiar toupper(getch( )) combination that retrieves an uppercase character from the keyboard.

The if test assigns x a value of zero if it is formerly equal to 'Y'. Likewise, x is assigned a value of one if it equates to 'N'. The else portion of this conditional operation takes over if neither a 'Y' nor 'N' are encountered. In such an instance, ct is incremented by 1 to access the next question, and the continue statement is used to cause the loop to recycle without executing further within the loop statement chain. This effectively bypasses the assignment statement that increments variable y.

On the other hand, if x is equal to 'Y', then the if statement causes it to be reassigned a value of 0. Then, when the y assignment line is reached, y is assigned a value equal to its current value plus the value contained at z[ct+ +][x]. On the first pass of the loop, variable y is equal to to 0. The first generation will be:

Does this animal have bones (Y/N/D)?

Let's assume you are asking the expert about a cat. The response to this question would be 'Y'. This would result in variable x being assigned a value of 0. Next, variable y would be incremented. A step in the incrementing would look like this:

y = y + z[0][0] or y = 0 + 0.33 or y = 0.33

The value of 0.33 occupies position 0,0 in the z array of double precision floating point values. This was the value that the human expert attributed to a positive answer to the first question. If the answer to this question has been 'N', then variable x would have been assigned a value of 1. This would have taken place within the if statement construct. Therefore, when it came time to increment variable y, the value in array z at position ct, x or 0,1 would have been accessed. This value would be −10.0 and would signal an immediate exit from the while loop. The reason for this latter occurrence lies in the fact that variable y is no longer more than −1.0. A decision can be made immediately. It is not necessary to ask further questions. If the animal has no bones, then it certainly is no mammal, because all mammals have bones.

Returning to the first example (remember, we're still asking about a cat), variable y is now equal to 0.33. This means that if the animal in question has bones, there is a predicted one-in-three chance that it could be a mammal. On the next pass of the loop, the question is:

Does this animal fly (Y/N/D)?

The answer to this question would be a definite 'N'. This results in variable x being assigned a value of 1. On this second pass of the loop, ct is now equal to 1. Variable y, which was previously assigned a value of 0.33, is incremented by the value found at position 1,1 in double precision floating point array z. This is the value of 0.25, which is what the human expert felt was appropriate for an animal that doesn't fly. Therefore, variable y is equal to 0.33 plus 0.25, or 0.58. There is now better than a 50 percent chance that an animal that has bones and doesn't fly is a mammal.

On the third pass of the loop, the question is:

Does this animal have a bill (Y/N/D)?

The response to this is also obviously 'N', but for the sake of this discussion, let's assume that you don't know whether or not a cat has a bill. The response, then, might be 'D'. This results in variable ct being incremented to the next question, but the incrementing of variable y does not take place. Therefore, this latter variable still equal to 0.58.

The next question is:

Does this animal have fur (Y/N/D)?

The answer to this question is 'Y', and this accesses a value of 0.75 in the array. Variable y is incremented by this amount and is now equal to 1.33. This brings about an immediate exit from the while loop because the value has exceeded +1.

At this juncture, it's time to evaluate our numerical results. The if condition chain is actually a rule for determination. In this example, variable y is tested for a value equal to or more than 1.0. This is true; therefore, the result clause residing at res[0] is displayed on the screen. This is the result which states that the animal in question is indeed a mammal.

All of the other possible results, with the exception of one, have already been discussed. If the numeric final total is more than or equal to 1, then it is a mammal. If it is less than or equal to −1, then the animal is not a mammal. If the number is positive but less than 1.0, then the animal is probably a mammal, and if the number is negative but more than −1.0, it is probably not a mammal. The only remaining condition is if the value should be equal to 0 exactly. This could happen, and the eventuality is planned for by one of the last program lines, which displays the "cannot determine" prompt.

Incidentally, very high values of +10.0 and −10.0 are used in the data base for positive eventualities. Even though a value of +1 or −1 is all that is required to determine a definite outcome, the high value makes up for any erroneous positive or negative values that may have resulted from answering any previous questions incorrectly. For instance, if the animal nurses its young, then it is a mammal. This is true regardless of how any of the other questions are answered. If the data base contained a value of +1.0 for answering this question with a 'Y' and if variable y was equal to −0.75, then the final total would be y = 0.25. The loop would not be exited immediately, even though the positive answer to the question was enough to decide the outcome. It is for this reason that an answer to a single question that stipulates a definite outcome is given a very high (10.0) negative or positive value. This brings about an immediate exit from the while loop for a speedier determination.

Certainly, one can argue with the numerical values that are attributed to each answer in this example. This is where it is necessary to have someone who is really expert in a field load the data base. This program will predict whether or not an animal is a mammal with good accuracy most of the time. You do run into problems when some of the answers are unknown and with certain specialized mammals. The duck-billed platypus comes to mind, as does the bat.

Another group of mammals that sometimes avoid detection are porpoises, dolphins, and the other beaked whales. Of course, these eventualities can and should be recognized ahead of time and special questions to overcome their anomalous results rebuilt into the program. Fortunately, the occurrence of such unusual mammals is mathematically small within the overall grouping of mammals, so programming for these special cases is a relatively easy task.

LEARNING BY TRIAL AND ERROR

Humans often think of the learning process as one of trial and error. The previous program did not need to go through such a procedure, but there are types of AI programs that do indeed learn by a system of making mistakes. It is up to the human expert to feed certain information to the program and then allow the computer to go through the motions of rendering a final determination. The computer would then ask if the outcome was correct—or incorrect. Based upon the response from the human expert, the system might try again and again until it arrives at the correct answer every time.

The program in FIG. 6-4 is an exercise in an expert system that actually learns by trial and error. It is closely akin to the previous program. However, for the sake of simplicity, the file keeping complexities have been omitted from this program. In describing its operation, I will stay within the realm of our previous problem, i.e., is it a mammal or is it not a mammal?

Fig. 6-4. This expert system learns by trial and error.

```c
main()
{
    int i, x, y, qrs[40], t[40];
    char ry[80], rn[80], f[80], e[40][80], num[20];
    printf("How many questions will be used? ");
    gets(num);
    y = atoi(num);
    for (i = 0; i < y; ++i) {
        qrs[i] = t[i] = 0;
        printf("Question #%d: ", i);
        gets(e[i]);
    }
    printf("\n\nName the first of two results\n");
    gets(ry);
    printf("Name the other result\n");
    gets(rn);
    while (ry) {
        for (i = 0 i < y; ++i) {
            qrs[i] = 0;
            printf("%s(Y/N)? ", e[i]);
            gets(f);
            if (tolower(f[0]) = 'y')
                qrs[i] = 1;
        }
        x = 0;
        for (i = 0; i < y; ++i)
            x += qrs[i] * t[i];
        if (x >= 0) {
            printf("The result is %s\n", ry);
            printf("Is this correct(Y/N)?\n");
            gets(f);
            if (tolower(f[0]) = 'y')
                continue;
            else
                for (i = 0 i < y; ++i)
                    t[i] -= qrs[i];
        }
        if (x < 0) {
            printf("The result is %s\n", rn);
            printf("Is this correct(Y/N)?\n");
            gets(f);
            if (tolower(f[0]) == 'y')
                continue;
            else
                for (i = 0 i < y; ++i)
                    t[i] += qrs[i];
        }
    }
}
```

Like the previous program, FIG. 6-4 assigns certain values to the elements of an array. In this example, however, the values are fixed at +1, −1, and 0. It is not necessary for a human expert to assign values to various questions, but the expert still must supply the needed questions.

When the program is executed, a prompt appears that asks for the total number of questions that will be asked. The human expert's response is read at the keyboard via the gets( ) function. The keyboard input is stored in char array num. Now, the atoi( ) function is used to retrieve the integer value from the string. Assuming that the prompt is responded to with a keyboard input of "7", atoi( ) will return the number 7 to variable y. The differentiation here is between the character '7' and the number 7.

The next operation involves a for loop which counts i from zero to one less than y. On each pass of the loop, the values in arrays qrs and t are initialized to zero. Remember, in C language, automatic variables are not initialized to any default value when declared. When an auto type variable is declared, it may be equal to any legal value. For our purposes, it is necessary that the array values be assigned an initial value of zero to provide a "clean slate" from which to perform our mathematical calculations. On each pass of this loop, the human expert is also asked to provide a question. The keyboard input is intercepted by the gets( ) function, which reads the information into char array e.

Now that the questions have been provided, a printf( ) function is used to display a prompt that asks for the first of two results. This particular program example is limited to only two different final conclusions. When the first result has been input, a prompt is provided to allow for inputting the second result. The results are stored in char arrays ry[ ] and rn[ ] (for result yes and result no), respectively.

A while loop is entered, from which all tutoring operations will take place. This is a test program used for demonstration purposes, and this while loop is an endless one. The argument to the loop is ry, which will never equate to zero; thus, the loop will continue cycling until execution is halted via a Ctrl−Break keyboard command. It would be a simple matter to place an exit clause within the while statement or to initialize an inner loop exit via the break statement or by using exit( ).

Within the while loop, a for loop is begun. Again, it counts variable i from zero to y − 1. Within this inner loop, qrs[ ] is assigned an initial value of zero. On the first pass of this loop, this assignment is redundant, because the same assignment was made within the first for loop of the program. On subsequent passes of this last for loop, this operation may be thought of as a reassignment, which is necessary to the functioning of the program.

Next, a printf( ) function is used in conjunction with e[i] asking if the description fits. This last variable is the one that contains the various descriptions. Therefore, on the first pass of the loop, the first description is displayed and the user must indicate whether or not the description is applicable to whatever they have in mind for one of the two results.

The user response is captured by the gets( ) function. Actually, all you are looking for is the first character in f[ ]. However, because gets( ) captures a string from the keyboard, the single character (Y/N) is terminated by a null character (\0), converting this to a bonafide one-character string.

The if statement line uses the tolower( ) function to convert the first character in character array f to lowercase. If the result is 'y', then qrs[i] is assigned a value of 1. If not, qrs[i] remains at a value of zero.

This inner for loop is now exited, and variable x is assigned a value of zero. Another inner for loop is begun, which counts i from 1 to the value of y. You will remember that variable y contains the number of descriptions that have been used for this particular program run. Only one statement is executed within this for loop. It increments variable x by the product of qrs[i] * t[i]. This operation forms a determination rule and allows the program to learn which values result in which results. More on this later.

The if statement line that follows tests to see if the value of variable x is more than or equal to zero. If so, a printf( ) function is used to display the result in char array ry. At this point, this is a purely arbitrary selection. The result contained in array ry may or may not be the result associated with an outcome of variable x being more than or equal to zero.

Another printf( ) function is used to write a screen prompt asking the user if this result is correct for the descriptions given. The user input is captured by the gets( ) function and assigned to array f as a string. An if statement line tests for a positive response. If this is the case, the continue statement causes the while loop to recycle. This allows the user to provide descriptions for the alternate result.

However, if the initial result displayed by the program is incorrect, the else portion of the if statement line takes over. It executes a for loop, which counts i from a to y. On each pass of this inner loop, t[i], which was initially assigned values of zero, is decremented by the value in qrs[i].

Now, if x had initially been less than zero (an impossibility on the first pass of the loop), another if statement line would detect this result. Before going further on this, look back to the beginning of the program and you will see that qrs[i] and t[i] are assigned values of zero. Within the while loop, qrs[i] may be assigned values of one if the description fits a particular result the user has in mind. However, in the determination rule line which increments x by qrs[i] * t[i], variable x will always be equal to zero (on the first pass only). This is due to the fact that while qrs[i] may have a positive value, t[i] still has a value of zero. Anything multiplied by zero results in zero. Therefore, during the first pass of the loop, variable x will always be equal to zero. The first if statement construct will read this result and make decisions accordingly.

Assuming that the arbitrary result which is displayed is not the desired one for the descriptions given, t[i] will be reassigned negative values or values of 0 based upon the values contained in qrs[i]. If one array position with qrs[ ] is equal to one, then this is subtracted from the current value in t[ ] and the result is the t[i] = = −1. However, if the value in qrs[i] is equal to 0, then the corresponding array position in t[i] will also equal 0.

On the next pass of the loop, the array elements in t[ ] may not all be equal to zero. You will again be asked to indicate whether or not the descriptions fit, and the corresponding values will be written to qrs[i]. On the second pass, it is assumed that variable x is decremented to a value of less than zero. Now, the second if statement construct at the bottom of the program takes over, and the user is asked whether or not the result found in array rn[ ] is correct. If so, the while loop recycles due to the continue statement. If not, t[i] is incremented by the value in qrs[i]. In the previous example, t[i] was decremented.

What occurs in actual operation is a continuous repeat of the descriptions. The user keeps in mind one of the two possible results as each of the descriptions is displayed. The program eventually learns which set of descriptions results in a value of variable x (more or less than zero) that identifies a specific outcome.

Make a sample run-through and teach your expert system the difference between a horse and a cow. Hopefully, it will be able to learn the rules that determine each and identify them when asked to do so by a user.

Five descriptions will be used, some of which apply only to a horse. Others apply only to cows, and still others apply to both horses and cows. The descriptions are:

1) Four legs
2) Horns
3) Farm animal
4) Nurse its young
5) Ride it

Before beginning, note that both horses and cows have four legs, only cows have horns, both are farm animals, both nurse their young, and only horses are ridden.

As you are given the first set of descriptions, assume you are thinking of a horse. The answers to whether or not the descriptions fit are y, n, y, y, y, respectively. This results in the array elements of qrs[ ] being equal to 1, 0, 1, 1, 1, respectively. The array elements in [ ] are all equal to zero.

The program detects the fact that variable x is more than or equal to zero, so the result in array ry (horse) is displayed. This is the correct response, so you respond with a 'y' when asked if the outcome is correct. The loop continues to cycle and the same descriptions are provided again. This time, you are thinking of a cow. The answers to the correctness of the above descriptions are y, y, y, y, n, respectively. This results in the values in qrs[ ] being equal to 1, 1, 1, 1, 0, respectively. On this second pass of the loop, the values in t[ ] are still 0. Variable x is still equal to 0. Therefore, the result in array ry (horse) is displayed again. Is this correct? The answer is no, so the second else portion of the first if statement construct takes over and decrements t[i] by the value found in qrs[i].

The loop cycles again. You again are thinking of a cow. The questions about description accuracy are answers in the same way again (1, 1, 1, 1, 0). Now, t[ ] is equal to − 1, − 1, − 1, − 1, 0. When variable x is incremented by qrs[i] * t[i], the result is negative value. Another if statement line detects this condition and displays the second possible result, which is found in array rn. COW is the correct answer.

Has the program learned yet? Not yet. You still must practice some more. On this pass, you are again thinking of a horse. The qrs[ ] array is loaded with 1, 0, 1, 1, 1; but now, t[ ] contains values other than zero. As a matter of fact, they are exactly the same values as were present during the last cycle (− 1, − 1, − 1, − 1, 0). The value in variable x, once all the descriptions have been provided, is still less than zero. The program asks if COW is the proper result. This is incorrect, so the else portion of the if statement construct increments each element in t[i] by the value in qrs[i].

Do it again. You are now thinking of a horse. The values in qrs[ ] are 1, 0, 1, 1, 1, and the values in t[ ] are now 0, − 1, 0, 0, 1. This is the first time t[ ] has contained all three of the possible values. Variable x is now equal to a positive value after all descriptions have been provided, and HORSE is the displayed result. This is correct.

Now try a cow. Here, qrs[ ] is equal to 1, 1, 1, 1, 0, and t[ ] is still equal to 0, − 1, 0, 0, 1. When qrs[i] * t[i] is used to increment variable x, the outcome is negative. This means the result is a COW, which is also correct.

By this trial and error method, the computer has been able to arrange its values in the t[ ] array in such a way as to always come up with with a positive value in variable x for the first result, and a negative value for the second. This is an excellent example of an artificial intelligence program that learns.

This particular program was set up to allow a maximum of 40 different descriptions but, of course, there can only be two outcomes. This is somewhat limiting in many applications, but in many others it may be just what the programmer ordered. Most of the programs in this book are designed for demonstration purposes, but many of them (this one included) can be put to practical application.

As is the case when teaching a small child to read, teaching a household pet to do tricks, or teaching experienced programmers a new language, the best concept to follow is that of *practice, practice, practice*. This is what has been done within this program to learn the difference between a horse and a cow. The user goes through the motions until the machine finally gets the hang of it. This certainly mimics many human learning experiences.

SAVING THE INFORMATION

Of course, this program would be a lot more practical if there were some way to save information that the program learned. As it is now, the program must be taught each time it is executed. If we terminate execution and run the program again, we would have to teach the horse/cow routine all over again.

However, once the program has been "taught", it is obvious that all of the needed information is stored in variables. It is a simple matter to "dump" this information to a permanent storage medium such as a disk drive. The program modification in FIG. 6-5 allows for the learned information to be saved.

This is the same program that was discussed previously, but a routine has been added that allows the learned information to be stored on disk, presumably to be called again in order to load the memory of a similar expert system. An escape line has been placed within the while loop that allows the user to exit the program. When the while loop is exited via a break statement), a prompt asks if the information is to be saved.

If the response to this prompt is yes, then three files are opened. These have been arbitrarily named result, dbase, and deter. The first file would hold the two possible results, and the second contains the

Fig. 6-5. This modification allows learning to be saved.

```c
#include <stdio.h>
main()
{
    int i, x, y, qrs[40], t[40];
    char ry[80], rn[80], f[80], e[40][80],num[20];
    FILE *fp, *fpp;

    printf("How many questions will be used? ");
    gets(num);

    y = atoi(num);

    for (i = 0; i < y; ++i) {
        qrs[i] = t[i] = 0;
        printf("Question #%d: ", i + 1);
        gets(e[i]);
    }

    printf("\n\nName the first of two results\n");
    gets(ry);
    printf("Name the other result\n");
    gets(rn);

    while (ry) {
        for (i = 0; i < y; ++i) {
            qrs[i] = 0;
            printf("%s(Y/N)? ", e[i]);
            gets(f);
            if (tolower(f[0]) == 'y')
                qrs[i] = 1;
        }

        x = 0;
        for (i = 0; i < y; ++i)
            printf("%d    %d\n", qrs[i], t[i]);
        for (i = 0; i < y; ++i)
            x += qrs[i] * t[i];

        if (x >= 0) {
            printf("The result is %s\n", ry);
            printf("Is this correct(Y/N)?\n");
            gets(f);
            if (tolower(f[0]) == 'y') {
                printf("Do you want to continue(Y/N) \n");
                if (tolower(getch()) == 'y')
                    continue;
                else
                    break;
            }
            else
                for (i = 0; i < y; ++i)
                    t[i] -= qrs[i];
        }
```

(Fig. 6-5 cont.)

```
            if (x < 0) {
                printf("The result is %s\n", rn);
                printf("Is this correct(Y/N)?\n");
                gets(f);
                if (tolower(f[0]) == 'y')
                    continue;
                else
                    for (i = 0; i < y; ++i)
                        t[i] += qrs[i];
            }
        }
    printf("Do you wish to save this data base(Y/N)?\n");
    gets(f);
    if (tolower(f[0]) == 'y') {
        fp = fopen("result", "w");
        fprintf(fp, "%s%s\n", ry, rn);
        fclose(fp);

        fp = fopen("dbase", "w");
        fpp = fopen("determ", "w");

        for (i = 0; i < y; ++i) {
            fputs(e[i], fp);
            fprintf(fpp, "%d %d\n", qrs[i], t[i]);
        }
        fclose(fp);
        fclose(fpp);
}
```

descriptions. The third contains the values for qrs[ ] and t[ ]. This information is written from the arrays directly to their respective files.

Although no program is shown that will load this information, it would be a very simple matter to open these files at the beginning of the program and read the information back into the respective arrays in reverse order of the above operation. No specific example is provided for this particular program because programs that are to follow in this chapter will perform these operations.

PATTERN RECOGNITION

The program in FIG. 6-6 allows you to build a data base, teach the system to recognize certain patterns, save the data base, and then reload it and use it again. This program does not work in exactly the same manner as the previous one, which assigns values for yes and no answers and then performs mathematical operations on these values. The program in FIG. 6-6 assigns values for yes and no answers, but it matches the patterns of the 1s and 0s that represent the yes and no answers to determine an outcome. You can say that the results of this program are the same as the previous one, but the way it arrives at these results is different and probably more accurate in most instances than the former.

The program in FIG. 6-6 is quite long and involved, but that shouldn't frighten anyone. The program is complex because it is designed to allow the user to build a data base, teach the rules of utilizing the data base, save the data base, or load the data base. You might think of this as four separate programs.

In order to enhance your understanding of the program, it will be discussed on a line by line basis, as has been the case of previous examples. To further facilitate understanding, this program is included in the appendices of this book with most lines commented. The comments that effect each line are sometimes numerous and can make the entire program look like a jumbled mess. For this reason, most programs are included in the chapters of this book without significant comments. Here, the text discussions take their place. However, for future reference, the commented program lines in the appendices can serve as a valuable study source.

When the program is executed, a puts( ) function is used to ask the user whether or not they want to construct the data base. This assumes that no data base is currently in place and one must be built from scratch. The response is read into variable x by using a combination of the toupper( ) and getch( ) functions. As was described earlier, this combination assures that the character (or integer value of the character) written to variable x will always be uppercase.

Assume that the response was positive, so the if statement line determines that variable x does indeed equal 'Y'. Statements tied to this if statement are then executed. First of all, variable y is initialized to zero. Then the user is prompted to type all questions that cover the subject area. Each of the questions is written to q[y]. The char array q[ ] was dimensioned to hold up to 100 different character strings of 100 characters each (99 text characters plus the NULL character).

To exit from this portion of the program, simply respond to the prompt for a question with "end". An if statement line within this while loop tests for the occurrence of "end" in q[y++]. This same line also increments variable y so that the next array position is available for writing should the current position not contain the exit keyword. When "end" is detected, a break statement causes the while loop to be exited.

Fig. 6-6. This program incorporates most expert systems basics.

```c
#include <stdio.h>
main()
{

    int i, x, y, z[100][100], zt[100];
    char q[100][100], c[240], res[100][100];
    FILE *fp, *fpp;

    puts("Do you want to construct the data base(Y/N)?");
    x = toupper(getch());

    if (x == 'Y') {
        y = 0;
        puts("Type all questions that cover the subject area.");
        while (y < 100) {
            printf("Question #%d = ", y + 1);
            gets(q[y]);
            if (strcmp(q[y++], "end") == 0)
                break;
        }

        printf("Press <return> to answer questions\n");
        x = getch();

        i = x = y = 0;
        while (strcmp(res[x], "end") != 0)
            while (y < 100) {
                printf("Name a result and answer the questions for that
                        result \n\n\n");
                printf("Result #%d = ", x + 1);
                gets(res[x]);
                if (strcmp(res[x], "end") == 0)
                    break;

                printf("\n\n\nAnswer the following questions about
                        <%s>.\n\n\n", res[x]);

                for (i = 0; strcmp(q[i], "end") != 0; ++i) {
                    printf("%s (Y/N)?", q[i]);
                    if (toupper(getch()) == 'Y')
                        z[x][i] = 1;
                    else
                        z[x][i] = 0;

                    printf("\n");
                }
                ++x;
            }

            fp = fopen("adbase", "w");
            fpp = fopen("adques", "w");
```

Expert Systems 131

(Fig. 6-6 cont.)

```c
        i = 0;
        while (strcmp(q[i - 1], "end") != 0)
            fprintf(fpp, "%s\n", q[i++]);

        fclose(fpp);

        i = x = y = 0;
        while (strcmp(res[x - 1], "end") != 0) {
            fprintf(fp, "%s\n", res[x]);
            if (strcmp(res[x], "end") == 0)
                break;

            for (i = 0; strcmp(q[i], "end") != 0; ++i)
                fprintf(fp, "%d", z[x][i]);

            fprintf(fp, "\n");
            ++x;
        }

        fclose(fp);
        printf("Data Base has been saved.\n");
    else {
        i = x = y = 0;
        printf("Do you wish to use the data base(Y/N)\n");
        x = toupper(getch());

        if (x == 'N') {
            printf("Data has been saved...exiting Expert.\n");
            exit(0);
        }

        if (x == 'Y') {
            if ((fp = fopen("adbase", "r")) == NULL) {
                printf("Cannot open data base\n");
                exit(0);
            }
            if ((fpp = fopen("adques", "r")) == NULL) {
                printf("Cannot access question file\n");
                exit(0);
            }

            for (x = 0; ; ++x) {
                fgets(q[x], 80, fpp);
                q[x][strlen(q[x])-1] = '\0';
                if (strcmp(q[x], "end") == 0)
                    break;
            }
            for (x = 0; ; ++x) {
                fgets(res[x], 80, fp);
                res[x][strlen(res[x]) - 1] = '\0';
                if (strcmp(res[x], "end") == 0)
                    break;
                fgets(c, 240, fp);

                for (i = 0; strcmp(q[i], "end") != 0; ++i)
                    z[x][i] = c[i] - '0';
```

(Fig. 6-6 cont.)

```
            }
            printf("Data base has been loaded into memory.\n");
        }
    }
    c[0] = '\0';   /* c == NULL */
    while (strcmp(c, "done") != 0) {
        printf("\n\n\n\n");
        printf("EXPERT\n\n");

        i = x = y = 0;

        while (strcmp(q[x], "end") != 0) {
            printf("%s (Y/N)? ", q[x]);
            y = toupper(getch());
            if (y == 'Y')
                zt[x++] = 1;
            else
                zt[x++] = 0;

            printf("\n");
        }

        for (x = 0; strcmp(res[x], "end") != 0; ++x) {
            y = 0;
            for (i = 0; strcmp(q[i], "end") != 0; ++i) {
                if (zt[i] != z[x][i]) {
                    y = 40;
                    break;
                }
                else y = 3;
            }

            if (y == 3)
                printf("The result is %s\n", res[x]);
        }

        if (y != 3)
            printf("The answer cannot be determined.\n");

        printf("\n\n\nDo you want to quit(Y/N)\n");
        x = toupper(getch());
        if (x == 'Y')
            strcpy(c, "done");

    }
}
```

Now that all the questions have been input, it's time to name one of two results and answer questions. Variables i, x, and y are initialized to zero. A while loop is entered. It continues to loop as long as res[x] is not equal to "end". This latter array can be used to hold up to 100 different results. Therefore, this program is not limited to only two results, as was the case with the previous example. Within this outer while loop, an inner while loop is established, which will test variable y for its value. As long as variable y is less than 100, the loop will continue to cycle, 100 being the maximum number of questions or results that this program can maintain.

Within the inner loop, the user is asked to name a result and answer the questions for that result. The user supplied result is captured from the keyboard via the gets( ) function and written to array res[x]. An if statement line checks for res[s] being equal to "end". If so, this portion of the program is exited.

When the first result is input, a prompt instructs the user to answer questions about this result. Another nested loop (triple deep looping) is entered. This is a for loop that counts variable i from zero on up. The exit clause within this loop may seem odd to beginning C language programmers. Normally, the second portion of a for loop states a high value (or a low value for decrementing loops) for the variable that is initialized by the first portion. When the variable exceeds these conditions, the loop is exited. However, this termination clause can really consist of anything, and this usage tells the loop to continue incrementing variable i and looping as long as "end" is not contained in q[i]. When this does occur, the loop is exited.

Within this loop, the question contained in q[i] is displayed along with a Y/N prompt. All of this is handled within the first printf( ) function line in the for loop. The user is asked whether or not this question applies to the result last input. The response is captured by another toupper( )/getch( ) combination found within an if statement line. If the result is positive, then a +1 is assigned to array position z[x][i]. The z array is used to contain the pattern of 1s and 0s that make up the value for any particular result. If the response is negative, then this same array position is assigned a value of zero. This loop continues to cycle until all questions have been asked about this particular result.

The for loop is then exited and the nested while loop cycles again. The user is asked for another result and the same questions are asked of this one. This pattern continues until "end" is given as a result. This brings about an exit from the outer while loop.

At this point, all database information is contained in program variables. It is time to write this information to a disk file for more permanent storage.

In the next two lines, FILE pointers *fp and *fpp are made to point disk files "adbase" and "adques", which have been opened for write operations. In this example, no check is made for a NULL return, which would be the case if these files could not be opened for some reason. This program is designed to demonstrate AI techniques and not to teach C language programming as such. However, each of these fopen( ) function lines should be nested within if statements that test for a NULL return upon attempting to open these files. If a NULL is returned, then the file could not be opened due to some malfunction, and the program should be exited. These protection lines are not presented here because they add to program complexity in an area that is of little benefit to teaching artificial intelligence techniques. In other words, the extra lines might further confuse the issue. Later program examples will include such protective features. Again, trying to open files without checking to make sure they have indeed actually been opened is poor programming practice.

Assume that the files have been successfully opened, so all that is necessary is to write the information from the appropriate variables into the appropriate files. For the purposes of this discussion, adbase is the file that contains the result and its associated pattern. The file named adques contains the questions, the answers to which are contained in the result patterns.

Initially, variable i is assigned a value of zero and a while loop is entered. This loop uses the fprintf( ) function to write information to the file named "adques". On each pass of the loop, a character string consisting of the question in q[i + +] is written to the open file. This loop continues to cycle until "end" is written to the file. When this has been done, q[i - 1] is equal to "end" and the loop is exited. Immediately, the fclose( ) function is used to close this file.

Another loop is entered which is used to write to the file named "adbase". This file contains three fprintf( ) functions. The first writes the result found in res[x] to one file line. An if statement line checks to make certain the result just written wasn't equal to "end". If so, the loop is exited. If not, a nested for loop is entered, which counts variable i from zero up to a value that corresponds to the array position that holds the exiting "end" escape word.

On each pass of this loop, one pattern value (1 or 0) from array z[ ] is written to the current file line. When the last pattern value is read in, fprintf( ) is called again to write the newline character to the file. This terminates a single file line. It should be understood that the adbase file arranges its information in groups of two lines. The first line contains the result, and the second contains the pattern for that result. This continues to the end of the file in a combination of result/pattern, result/pattern, result/pattern, etc.

When the for loop is exited (after a full pattern has been written), it is exited and control returns to the outer while loop. Another result is written to the file and another pattern. When all results and patterns have been written to disk, the while loop is exited and fclose( ) is called again to close the adbase file. A prompt tells the user that all information has been saved.

At this point in the program, else appears, seemingly from out of nowhere. This is the portion of the opening if statement line that tested the user's response to the question "Do you want to construct the data base?" If the response had been negative, then the else portion of the if statement would have taken over. Skip over this section of code for right now so that you can stay within the execution sequence that would occur if you had constructed the data base in the manner just described. It will be necessary for you to skip down to the portion of the program that starts with:

$c[0] = '\0';$

This is where execution continues following the proper loading of the data base. A while loop is immediately entered that cycles as long as "done" is not contained in array c[ ]. Within this loop, a couple of printf( ) functions display the EXPERT logo. Next, variables i, x, and y are initialized to zero.

It is at this point that the expert system is really put to use. All previous operations simply taught our idiot savant expert to be less than an idiot. A nested while loop is entered, which prints the first question in array q[ ]. Assume that the user has a need to know a result based upon certain questions to which they know the answer. The user is prompted to answer the first question asked with a positive or negative response. In other words: "Does this question pertain to the result you have in mind?" On each pass of the loop, a pattern based upon the user's input is written to array zt[x + +]. This pattern consists of 1s and 0s, as was the case with previous patterns discussed. However, this pattern is supplied by a supposedly non-expert user who is simply answering questions. This is not to be confused with the patterns that were coupled with any particular result.

When all questions have been answered, the nested while loop is exited and a nested for loop is entered. This one searches through the res[ ] array. It does this by initializing variable y to a value of 0 within the loop and then entering another nested loop, which counts variable i from 0 up to a value that represents all patterns. On each pass of the triple-nested loop, each value in the user-supplied pattern contained in zt[i] is compared with a data base pattern value connected with the result contained in the current res[ ] array position. As long as the pattern values continue tinue to match, the triple-nested for loop continues to cycle. However, an if statement line within this triple-nested loop constantly looks for a mismatch between the two. If this occurs, it assigns variable y an arbitrary value of 40 and executes a break statement that causes this triple-nested loop to be exited.

Make certain you understand this aspect of the program. The user answers questions. Each yes answer adds a one to the pattern. Each no answer adds a zero. It there are 40 questions, then the pattern consists of 40 values of 1s and 0s. Within the triple-nested for loop, each of these (40) values contained in the user pattern is compared with each of 40 values contained in a data base pattern that is coupled with the result. If any one comparison fails, then the program assumes that the result the data base pattern is associated with is not the proper one. Therefore, the nested loop is exited and the outer for loop takes control by bringing up another result and its matching pattern for comparison with the user pattern. Variable y is assigned a value of 40 because its value is used to determine when an answer has been reached.

Whenever the value in the user pattern matches the corresponding value in the data base pattern, the else portion of the if clause assigns variable y a value of 3. This occurs when any single element match is found. However, when a mismatch is found, the outer for loop takes over and reassigns variable y a value of zero. Therefore, variable y may be equal to 0, 3, or 40, depending upon the match outcome.

When a perfect match is found, variable y is equal to 3 and the result is displayed on the screen. If, however, no match is found, then variable y would be equal to 40. This means that the user's pattern did not match any pattern within the data base and the computer displays the "cannot determine" prompt. This indicates that the user has either not answered the questions correctly or is looking for a result not contained within the data base. At this juncture, the user is asked if they wish to continue or exit the program. If the response is to exit, then "done" is copied to array c using the strcpy( ) function. This is detected by the outer while loop and program execution is terminated.

This program has been discussed from beginning to end. However, there was a section in the middle that was purposely skipped over. To fully explore this section, assume that everything already discussed has occurred. The data base has been loaded, the expert system used, and execution has been terminated. Now run the program again, but this time, when asked if you wish to construct the data base, the response is negative.

Here is where the else portion of the if-else clause at the beginning of the program takes over. This is the section of the program that begins with:

```
else {
    i = x = y = 0;
```

Assuming that the user doesn't wish to construct a data base, prompt appears asking if the user wishes to use the data base. If the response to this prompt if 'N', then the program is exited. Otherwise, the information contained in files "adbase" and "adques" is read into memory. This next sequence uses proper procedures in opening files via C language calls, in that tests are made using if statement constructs to make certain that the files really are open. This is proper programming procedure.

The first if statement line causes FILE pointer *fp to point to "adbase", which is opened for read only operations. Because it is nested within an if statement line, the value assigned to *fp is tested. If it is equal to NULL, then a printf( ) statement tells the user that the data base cannot be accessed and the program is exited. After all, there's no reason to continue with a program that must utilize data base information if the data base file cannot be opened, perhaps due to some disk or machine error.

The same procedure is used in opening "adques". This file is also opened for read only operations and is accessed via FILE pointer *fpp.

Assume that both files have been successfully opened. It is now necessary to read the information from each file and place it into the correct array. A for loop is established for this purpose. This loop may also look strange to beginning C programmers, in that it contains no exit clause. This area of the normal for construct is blank. This is an endless loop. It initializes variable x to a value of zero and then tells it to keep on cycling and continue incrementing variable x by one on each pass. This loop will continue to cycle on to infinity if some internal exit is not programmed. As you would expect, an internal exit does exist. More on this later.

On each pass of this loop, the fgets( ) function is called to get a line from the open file. In this case, the FILE pointer argument is *fpp, which points to "adques". Other arguments to fgets( ) include q[x], the array that holds the questions, and an integer constant value of 79. This last value tells fgets( ) to read a maximum of 79 characters. This array was dimensioned for lines a maximum of 80 characters in length. By specifying 79 as the maximum number of characters that can be read into the array, room is left for the NULL character terminator. This effectively fills the array to its maximum.

Now, chances are that fgets( ) will never get to read a full 99 characters because there will be fewer characters than that on each line. The fgets( ) function will read up to the maximum number of characters specified, or until it reaches a newline character n. The newline signals termination of the file read for that particular line. You may have notices that when writing information to the file, which was discussed previously, each file write was concluded by a newline character. This signals the end of the line.

When fgets( ) reads a new line, it appends it to the character string already read and then terminates with a NULL \0, making it a bonafide string. It is necessary to use the newline character to separate lines, but the newline, when written to the screen, produces a carriage return and advancement to the next screen line. It is advantageous to write new lines to files for differentiation purposes, but the same new line can be a real hindrance when read from a file because it can affect on-screen displays.

For this reason, an assignment line follows the fgets( ) function, which erases the newline character from the string. It does this by overwriting it with a NULL character. The NULL signals the end of a character string.

This assignment:

q[x] [strlen(q[x]) - 1] = '\0';

may be a bit confusing. Before you can overwrite the newline with a NULL, it is necessary to find out where it is in the string. It is already known that it will be the second to the last character, because the last character in any C language string must necessarily be '\0' or NULL. The strlen( ) function returns the number of characters in a string. This character count, however, does not include the NULL character. Therefore, if a string is composed of "THE\0", then strlen( ) will return a count of 3, because there are three characters in "THE". However, if a string is composed of "THE\n\0", strlen( ) will return a value of 4, which is the number of characters other than the NULL in the string. Again, '\n' represents the newline character.

In the last example, strlen( ) has returned a value of 4, which is the character count in the string. However, in C language, strings are written on a character-by-characters basis to advancing array positions in a character array variable. Therefore, given this example, 'T' is written to array position 0, 'H' to position 1, 'E' to position 2, and the newline ('\n') to position 3. Therefore, the actual position at which the newline is written is equal to:

strlen("THE\n\0' - 1

This is the strlen() return minus one. This is exactly what is done in the assignment line under discussion. Array q[ ] is a multi-dimensional type. Therefore, the first bracket value contains the line number, while the second contains the elements of that line. It is the second dimension that must be accessed in order to overwrite the newline character. Therefore, the second set of brackets contain an argument that is the equivalent of the length of line q[x] minus 1. This names the offset into the array where the newline is written. This character is replaced with the NULL, and our newline problems are over. Remember, the newline is written on purpose as a termination indicator for the end of a file line. It is eliminated when it is read back into an array because it is no loner needed and, in fact, causes problems.

Within the for loop, and if statement line checks for the presence of q[x] being equal to "end". When this occurs, the loop is exited, but only after "end" is written to the last array position.

The loop is exited via a break statement. This is the internal termination or exit referred to a bit earlier. Without this break statement, the loop would continue to cycle to infinity. Naturally, if your data base file does not contain the "end" exit word, the loop will continue to cycle.

At this juncture, the data base questions have been fully loaded into array q[ ]. This array now contains the same information it did when the data base was completely written during a previous operation. Another for loop is called in the same manner as the previous one, but this one reads in the result information from the file named adbase.

Again, fgets( ) is used to read in the information. However, in this loop, fgets( ) is used twice. You will remember that this file contained information that was written in two-line segments of result/pattern, result/pattern, etc. The first call to fgets( ) reads the result into array res[ ]. Another assignment line nearly identical to the one previously discussed overwrites the newline character with a NULL. Following this, an if statement line checks for the presence of "end" in the array. If so, a break statement brings about an internal exit from this endless loop. If the end of the file has not been reached, however, fgets( ) is called again to read a second file of information

The entire pattern in this second line is read to char array c. Now, a for loop is entered that counts from zero to (effectively) one less than the total number of questions contained in q[ ]. On each pass of this loop, one character from c is transferred to array z[ ].

Now, array c contains a bonafide character string. There are no numbers in this string, only characters. Even though the characters may be 1s and 0s, these are not the number 1 and the number 0, but rather, the characters that represent them. Again, these are not numbers,but characters. For instance, if you assign a variable a value of 1, then it indeed is equal to 1. However, if you assign this same variable a value of '1', then this variable is equal to the character '1', which equates to a numeric or ASCII value of 49. Therefore, the assignment line:

x = '1';

is identical to:

x = 49;

They both assign x the exact same value.

Now the problem: You have a pattern in c which consists of the characters for the numbers you wish to transfer to numeric array z[ ]. How do you go about doing this?

Some beginners might suggest using the atoi( ) or atof( ) function. That's a good guess, but these functions are designed to extract whole numeric quantities from a string. You don't want to do that in this case because the pattern doesn't represent a whole numeric quantity. Rather, each element of the pattern represents a single numeric quantity.

There's an easy way to accomplish this. Taking the above example a step backward, the assignment line:

x = '0';

is identical to:

x = 48;

In other words, the ASCII value for '0' is 48. Now, by subtracting '0' from any character that represents the numbers 0-9, we end up with the numeric value which that character represents. The following demonstrates this principle:

x = '1' - '0'

This assigns variable x a value of numeric 1. This is not the character '1', but the number 1. By substituting ASCII values for the two characters in the above assignment line, the answer is clearer:

x = 49 - 48;

With this in mind, the assignment line within the nested for loop assigns z[x][i] a value of the character in c[i] - '0'. This effectively converts the numeric characters in the array to individual numbers.

When this loop is exited for the last time, the data base information constructed during an earlier operation is now back in resident memory, and the user proceed on to the portion of the program that evokes the expert system.

Though this explanation of how information is loaded into resident memory, and converted to suit the program's various requirements, is quite long, the operation takes place in a few seconds. The difficulties involved here include removing the unwanted newline character and converting a string of 1s and 0s that are characters into the equivalent numbers that can be assigned to numeric array elements.

This program works quite well and is always accurate, as long as the questions are answered in an accurate manner. The following list is the adbase file created by this program. Staying with our animal format, these expert system was taught to identify animals such as bats, birds, turtles, and snakes by answering the questions presented. The adbase file contains the result names followed by the corresponding pattern:

BAT
0101100110
BIRD
0000110110
TURTLE
1000000111
SNAKE
1000000100
end

The next list shows the corresponding question file (adques) that was used to build the above numeric patterns:

Scales
Fur
Hump
Nurses Young
Flies
Feathers
Breathes through gills
Bones
Warm blooded
Has a shell
end

Obviously, it would be possible to build up quite a comprehensive data base using this simple AI program. However, it would be terribly time-consuming. Nor do even highly sophisticated AI programs offer any significant advantage in the speed of building a data base. The data base information must be put in by an expert and all questions pertaining to the results must be anticipated.

However, many expert systems are designed to learn as they work. For instance, if a desired result is not contained in the data base, the program might prompt the user that the information is not available. An expert could then take over and add to the data base during the middle of its operation, as opposed to running another program designed purely to build a data base.

For an expert system animal identifier, this type of operation might be evidenced by the expert system guessing that the animal you were describing was a goat instead of the deer you had in mind. The system might ask for the name of the animal you were describing and then ask the user to input a question that would differentiate the deer from the goat. One of the first AI programs I ever used was written in LISP and did just that.

EXPERT GUESSING

The following discussions involve a program or, more accurately, a set of programs that evolved directly from the one just discussed. The example to follow are set up to allow animal identification based upon the user answering some questions. It may seem a bit elementary to be discussing a program that tries to guess the animal the user is thinking of, but this is the same scenario used over and over again with expert systems. In a more environment, the program might be trying to guess what is wrong with a doctor's patient based upon the answers to some medical questions in the system's data base.

Of course, the word "guess" seems inappropriate. For many of the expert systems discussed so far, it is. However, what is a guess? In human terms, it can be defined as a wild stab in the dark at an answer that is correct. How wild and how far in the dark is a matter for conjecture. However, in purer terms, a *guess* is an inference based upon incomplete data. Expert systems can and do make such inferences.

Naturally when designing such a system, it is preferable to have discovered all of the variables and made allowances for them, but it is also necessary to allow the program to make inferences based upon the direction in which the data base is pointing when the exact determination of an answer broke down. You have seen such examples earlier in this chapter with a program that identified a mammal (or not a mammal) based upon user input. If the input was incomplete and a determination could not be made, the program made a guess by outputting an answer like "this animal is probably a mammal" or "this animal is probably not a mammal".

In the following example, we are trying to rule out probabilities altogether. In other words, the program depends upon a complete recognition pattern to output any answer. If the pattern is not complete, then an answer cannot be output. This can later be built up to yield some very nice possibilities. More on this aspect later.

The program in FIG. 6-7 is designed to identify animals. The only thing that limits it to this purpose is the abundance of prompts that mention animals. Change these and the program could identify vegetables, medical problems, etc. The first program is designed to build a data base and to "teach" the system. The second program is designed to load the already-constructed data base and to allow access to the user portion of the expert system.

Again, the program in FIG. 6-7 is designed to allow an expert to build a data base, or to add to one already in existence. You should notice that there are similarities in the declaration lines of this program to the declaration lines in the previous one discussed.

When the program is executed, multi-dimensional arrays quesm[ ] and creature[ ] are initialized to '\0' on an element-by-element basis. This "clears the deck," so to speak, and allows other portions of the program to detect when all questions or all results have been scanned. Without this initialization, the values randomly assigned to these array elements during declaration would confuse the entire program.

An endless loop is entered—one which will be exited by an internally called break statement. Within the loop, a prompt asks the expert user to input an animal. Due to the way the program that will eventually read this information is constructed, it is essential that the animal name be one word, such as "elephant" as opposed to "bull elephant". If a two word name is necessary, separate the words with asterisks(*), dashes(-), etc.

The user response to this prompt is captured by the gets( ) function and read into animal[ ]. The Turbo C strupr( ) function is now called. This function simply converts all letters in its string argument to uppercase. Should some letters already by in uppercase, they are left unchanged.

Once the animal name is input, this program searches through its data base, looking for a previous occurrence of this animal. This search is conducted within a while loop. The loop cycles until creature[y][0] = = '\0'. This null character marks the end of the data base chain. Within the loop, an if statement construct tests for a match between the animal name just input by the user and an animal that has been previously typed into the data base. If a match is found, a prompt tells the user that the animal has already been input, variable y is assigned a value of −1 and a break statement is executed, terminating the loop.

Fig. 6-7. This program can be modified to identify anything.

```c
/* Teaching program for animal identification */

#include <stdio.h>
main()
{
    char creature[100][100];
    char quesm[100][100], name[30], code[200], fname[30];
    char *p, *f, question[100], animal[40], c[100], d[10];
    int i, k, q, x, y, z;
    FILE *fp, *fpp;

    for (x = 0; x < 100; ++x)
        quesm[x][0] = creature[x][0] = '\0';

    for (x = 0; ; ++x) {
        printf("Name an animal that is not a part of the data base: ");
        gets(animal);
        strupr(animal);

        y = 0;
        while (creature[y][0] != '\0') {
            if (strncmp(creature[y++], animal, strlen(animal)) == 0) {
                printf("Animal already exists in data base\n");
                y = -1;
                    break;
            }
        }

        if (y == -1) {
            --x;
            continue;
        }

        strcpy(creature[y], animal);

        printf("Type a question that pertains to the %s\n", animal);
        gets(question);
        strupr(question);

        y = 0;
        while (strcmp(creature[y], animal) != 0) {
            printf("\n\n%s:\n%s(Y/N)? ", creature[y], question);
            z = toupper(getch());
            if (z == 'Y')
                z = 1;
            else if (z == 'N')
                z = 0;
            else {
                --y;
                continue;
            }
```

Expert Systems

(Fig. 6-7 cont.)

```
            sprintf(c, "%d", z);
            strcat(creature[y++], c);
      }
      i = y;
      strcpy(quesm[y], question);
      strcat(creature[y], " ");
      for (y = 0; quesm[y][0] != '\0'; ++y) {
            printf("\n\n%s:\n%s(Y/N)", animal, quesm[y]);
            z = toupper(getch());
            if (z == 'Y')
                  z = 1;
            else if (z == 'N')
                  z = 0;
            else {
                  --y;
                  continue;
            }
            sprintf(c, "%d", z);
            strcat(creature[i], c);
      }
      printf("\n\nContinue(Y/N)?\n");
      z = toupper(getch());
      if (z == 'N') {
            fp = fopen("creature.dat", "a");
            fpp = fopen("quesm", "a");
            for (x = 0; creature[x][0] != '\0'; ++x) {
                  fprintf(fp, "%s\n", creature[x]);
                  fprintf(fpp, "%s\n", quesm[x]);
            }
            fclose(fp);
            fclose(fpp);

            break;
      }
            }
}
```

The next line executed is the y statement that checks the value of variable y. If y = = 0 then there is no problem and execution can continue. However, if y = = −1, then the animal just input is already in the data base, so the value of x, the loop variable is decreased by one and the continue statement is executed which causes this for loop to cycle again. When the new cycle is begun, variable x is incremented by one, so its value is back to where it was when the duplicate animal was input. The user gets another chance to input an animal not already stored in its data base.

If the animal input by the user is not already in the data base, then this name is written to creature[y] via the strcpy( ) function. The next order of business is to input a question that pertains to the animal just input. A prompt instructs the user to do this and gets( ) writes the user string to char array animal[ ]. Again strupr[ ] is used to convert all letters in question[ ] to uppercase.

Next comes the learning or teaching portion of the program. A while loop is entered and each creature in the data base is written to the screen, followed by the question just input. The user must then declare whether the question is true or false for all creatures in the data base. To make this operation clear, let's walk through the inputting of two animals and two questions:

Prompt:Name an animal not a part of the data base: CAT
Prompt:Type a question that pertains to the CAT

DOES IT PURR

Prompt:CAT
     DOES IT PURR(Y/N)?
User response: Y

Prompt:Name an animal not a part of the data base: DOG
Prompt:Type a question that pertains to the DOG

DOES IT BARK

Prompt:CAT
     DOES IT PURR(Y/N)?
User response: N

Prompt:DOG
     DOES IT BARK(Y/N)?
User response: Y

Prompt:DOG
     DOES IT PURR(Y/N)?
User response: N

You can see that each question is asked of all the animals in the data base. Any answer to a single question is checked against how this same question was asked of every animal in the data base. The while loop asks the question just typed of every animal in the data base. When this single question has been answered, it is necessary to ask all previous questions of the animal just input.

Once the while loop is exited, a for loop is entered that calls up every question in the data base and asks how it pertains to the creature just input. Put simply: whenever a new creature and question are added to the data base, all creatures must be asked the question most recently typed, and all questions previously typed must be asked of the new creature.

During the operation of both loops, a 'Y' equates to a value of 1 and an 'N' equates to a value of 0. The sprintf( ) function is used to write these values to c[ ] as characters (i.e.) '0' and '1'. What you are doing is constructing a character string from purely numeric quantities.

The control string argument to sprintf( ) is %d, which tells the function to expert an integer argument, which the numbers 0 and 1 truly are. However, when they are written to the char array and terminated by the null character, this combination becomes a string of character values. The former numbers are now individual characters.

Actually, sprintf( ) in this operation constructs strings composed on a single character as in "0\0" or "1\0". The null (\0) terminator makes these true strings rather than a series of characters. Next, the standard strcat( ) function is used to write the string contents in c[ ] to the end of the string contents of creature[ ]. The first part of array creature[ ] contains the name of the animal followed by a space. The pattern of 1s and 0s that identify this creature are added to the end of this array line a character at a time. So you would end up with something like:

DOG 10100010010010001

This is the way each and every item in the data base is added. When the first animal is input, a single question is asked. The loop cycles again and a second animal is input along with its question. This question is asked of the animal previously input, and of the latest animal. The previous question is asked of the latest animal. This sequence continues until all input operations are ended by typing 'N' as a response to the CONTINUE(Y/N)? prompt. Caution: This program is set up to hold a maximum of 100 animals and 100 questions. The endless loop that controls the input operations does not have an exit clause that terminates looping when this value is reached. This could easily be added as in:

    for (x = 0; x < 100; ++x)

instead of:

    for (x = 0; ; ++x)

This safety feature was not included with this program listing because such a program might be used to build a data base of several thousand items. In such a case, the array sizes would be made many times larger than they currently are for this demonstration program. If you should try to write to an array that is filled, memory areas not reserved for storage may be overwritten resulting in possible program interruption, and a myriad of general malfunctions.

When all animals and questions have been input, type 'N' to the CONTINUE(Y/N)? prompt and the endless for loop is exited. However, before the exit occurs, two disks files are opened. Again, this is a demonstration program and the safety features of checking to make certain that the files are actually opened have been disregarded in this instance. The previous warnings about this apply equally here.

Notice that the files are opened for append ("a") operations. This assures that data already stored in these files will be added to and not erased, as would be the case if the files were opened for write ("w") operations. If the two files do not exist on disk, then opening them for append will cause them to be created just as if they were open for write.

A for loop is entered and fprintf( ) functions are used to write the animal names and patterns (creature[ ]) and the questions (quesm[ ]) to their appropriate files. When the writes are completed, both files are closed via two fclose( ) functions. A break statement then causes the loop to be exited and execution terminates with the program's end.

To be a bit more flexible, it would be nice to build in a "front door" to this program that would allow the current file contents of "creature.dat" and "quesm" to be loaded into memory before the beginning operations take place. This could be easily added the way as that described in the last program. The two files would be opened, loaded into their proper arrays (get rid of those newline characters), and the program can then begin where it did before. It would be necessary to build in a routine at the opening of the endless for loop to count through to the end of the quesm[ ] array. This would be the point where the new information would be written. A routine such as:

```
if (quesm[x][0] != '\0')
    continue;
```

would cause the loop to cycle until the end of the list was reached. These additions would cause the program to load the current data base contents, count through to the last result/last question, and then allow the user to add to the data base.

Of course, the program as presented opens the files for append—so no current data base contents would be erased. However, all animals would not be subject to the same set of questions and, of course, animals could be input two or more times without adequate checks if the name already appears in the data base on disk. As presented, this program is best used to construct a single data base in one sitting.

Now that the data base has been built, it is necessary to come up with a program that will load the information from disk into current memory, and then allow a non-expert user to take advantage of this information and the rules for arriving at an outcome. The source code for just such a program is shown in FIG. 6-8. This program includes the Expert System, proper, which is the program portion that allows a non-expert access to its learned knowledge. However, before this access can be granted, it is necessary for the expert system to load its resident memory with the facts and rules previously loaded into its data base.

As before, a for loop is used to assign all array elements in quesm[ ] and in creature[ ] an initial value of 0. Next, a prompt is printed which asks if the Expert System is to be used. This prompt appears to be unnecessary and it is, but this program was "cut away" from a much larger program for the purposes of this discussion. This prompt is necessary when use in the body of the larger program which offers several more options than does this one.

If the response to the prompt is 'N', then the program is exited. Any other response causes the code under control of "else" to be executed. First of all, "creature.dat" is opened for read-only operations. Notice that the necessary precautions are taken to make certain the file is really available. If it can't be opened, a prompt explains the situation and the program is exited.

Assuming that the first file has successfully been opened, an identical routine is used to open the question file, "quesm". Now that both files have been opened for read-only operations, it is necessary to read their data into the proper arrays for use by the expert system.

A while loop is entered and the fgets( ) function is utilized to read information from "creature.dat" into array creature[ ]. A familiar routine is used to overwrite the newline character ($\backslash$n) with a null character ($\backslash$0). This was discussed previously. When creature[ ] is fully loaded, fgets( ) is used again to load the questions from the file named "quesm" into an array of the same name. Again, the newline is overwritten with a null character.

Both files are closed when these operations are completed. Now, the expert system has a memory and a brain. System operations may now take place.

The Expert System logo is written to the screen and variable end is assigned an initial value of 0 (zero). This will serve as an exit variable to allow a smooth exit from the Expert System. A while loop controls expert system operations, and the system may be used as long as the loop cycles. When the value in end is changed from zero to any other number, the loop is exited and the program is ended.

Fig. 6-8. It loads its database from disk.

```c
#include <stdio.h>
main()
{
    char creature[100][100];
    char quesm[100][80], name[30], code[200], fname[30];
    char *p, *f, question[100], animal[40], c[100], d[10];
    int i, k, q, x, y, z, end;
    FILE *fp, *fpp;

    for (x = 0; x < 100; ++x)
        quesm[x][0] = creature[x][0] = '\0';

    puts("Do you wish to use the Expert System(Y/N)?\n");
    x = toupper(getch());
    if (x == 'N')
        exit(0);
    else {
        if ((fp = fopen("creature.dat", "r")) == NULL) {
            puts("Cannot open data base file");
            exit(0);
        }
        if ((fpp = fopen("quesm", "r")) == NULL) {
            puts("Cannot open data base question file");
            exit(0);
        }

        x = 0;
        while ((fgets(creature[x], 100, fp)) != NULL) {
            creature[x][strlen(creature[x]) - 1] = '\0';
            ++x;
        }

        fclose(fp);

        x = 0;
        while ((fgets(quesm[x], 100, fpp)) != NULL) {
            quesm[x][strlen(quesm[x]) - 1] = '\0';
            ++x;

        }

        fclose(fpp);

    }
    printf("                         EXPERT SYSTEM\n\n");
    printf("                           ANIMALS\n\n\n");
    end = 0;
    while (end == 0) {
        c[0] = d[0] = name[0] = fname[0] = code[0] = '\0';
        i = q = x = y = 0;
        for (x = 0; quesm[x][0] != '\0'; ++x) {
```

Expert Systems 151

(Fig. 6-8 cont.)

```
                    printf("\n\n%s(Y/N)? ", quesm[x]);
                    y = toupper(getch());
                    if (y == 'Y')
                            y = 1;
                    else if (y == 'N')
                            y = 0;
                    else {
                            --x;
                            continue;
                    }
                    sprintf(d, "%d", y);
                    strcat(c, d);

                    i = 0;
                    for (z = q; creature[z][0] != '\0'; ++z) {
                            sscanf(creature[z], "%s %s", name, code);
                            if (strncmp(c, code, strlen(c)) == 0) {
                                    ++i;
                                    if (i == 1) {
                                            strcpy(fname, name);
                                    }
                                    else if (i == 2) {
                                            i = 0;
                                            break;
                                    }
                            }
                    }
                    if (i == 1)
                            break;
            }

            if (fname[0] == '\0')
                    printf("\n\n\nThis animal is not in my data bank\n");
            else
                    printf("\n\n\nI believe you have described %s.\n", fname);

            printf("\n\nDo you wish to continue(Y/N)?%c\n", 7);

            x = toupper(getch());
            if (x == 'N')
                    end = 1;

    }
}
```

Within this while loop, single dimension char arrays are initialized to null (\0). Next, several integer variables are assigned values of 0. A nester for loop is begun that will cycle until the end of the question list is reached (quesm[x][0] = = '\0').

152   Chapter 6

Remember, this program is designed to determine an animal the user has in mind by processing the user's answers to the questions contained in the expert system data base. Within the for loop, printf( ) is used to display the first question (quesm[0]). The user must respond with a 'Y' or a 'N'. Again, the 'Y' equates to a value of 1 in variable y, while a 'N' response causes variable y to be assigned a value of 0 (zero). If the response is other that 'Y' or 'N', the loop variable x is decremented by one, and a continue statement is executed causing the loop to cycle once more. On this cycle, variable x is incremented by 1, so the same question is asked again.

On each loop pass, the value in variable y is written to char array d[ ] as a string (i.e. "1\0" "0\0" "0\0" "1\0", etc.). Then, the strcat( ) function is used to concatenate each of these mini-strings onto the end of char array c[ ]. The end result is a pattern consisting of 1s and 0s.

Now, to this point, the operation of this program has seemed nearly identical to an earlier program that arrived at conclusions based upon pattern comparisons. The rule this one uses is often faster than the one used previously. The other program which used pattern matches asked all questions in its data base and then named the result. This one is more efficient. It checks for pattern mismatches before a full pattern has been established.

On each pass of the nested for loop, a pattern element (1 or 0) is added to char array c[ ]. On the first pass of the loop, c will contain a single pattern element. For the sake of this discussion, let's assume that the element is 1. Now, another nested for loop (triple nesting) is entered. On the first pass of the outside for loop, this nested for loop counts from z = q or zero upward until the end of the creature array is discovered. On each pass of this triple nested loop, the sscanf( ) function is used to extract the animal name from creature[z], and the pattern code from the second portion of the same array line. For instance, the line is creature[0] might read:

DOG 1010110001100110

The sscanf( ) function will write DOG to array name[ ] and will write the pattern code to array code[ ]. This is the reason why it was stressed that the animal name had to consist of a single word not separated by spaces. The sscanf( ) function stops scanning when it encounters a space character.

Now, there is name[ ] which contains DOG, code[ ] 1010110001100110, and c[ ] which contains 1. The if statement line that follows makes a comparison of the element(s) in c[ ] with the same number of elements in code[ ]. It accomplishes this by using the Turbo C strncmp( ) function, a derivative of strcmp( ) used earlier. The former function works just like the latter in comparing two strings on a character by character basis. However, strncmp( ) has a third argument that specifies the maximum number of characters to compare. If the number of characters in the strings is more than this maximum value, only the specified number of characters are compared.

For the third argument to strncmp( ), the strlen( ) function is called. This returns the number of characters in c[ ]. During the initial pass of the far outside loop, c[ ] == "1", therefore, strlen(c) == 1 . . . therefore, strncmp(c, code, strlen(c)) is the same as strncmp(c, code, 1). The end result as the loop continues to cycle is that the exact number of characters in c[ ] at any one time are compared with the same number of characters in code[ ].

Like strcmp( ), the strncmp( ) function returns 0 (zero) as the strings match, and negative or positive values if the first string is smaller than the second or larger than the second, respectively. All we are concerned with here is a match for a return of 0 (zero).

Each time an element match is found, variable i is incremented by one. The value in variable i is used as a determination factor for the portions of the program that follow. This variable can be thought of as a switch. When in one position, it means one thing—when in another position, it means another.

An if-else construct checks the value in variable i. If i == 1, then the animal name associated with the current pattern being tested against the user pattern is copied to fname[ ] using the strcpy( ) function.

The fname[ ] array is the one that will contain the name of the animal the expert arrives at as being the one described by the user. At this juncture, the animal name stored in fname[ ] may be only temporary. Because this copy only takes place when i == 1, this means that the first pass of the for loop for this particular animal and pattern yielded a match between the first element of the user's pattern and the first element of the data base pattern. Remember, the outside for loop counts through the elements in each pattern.

However, whenever a new pattern element is brought up, this is added to the pattern contained in c[ ]. The pattern is built an element at a time. The nested for loop counts through the animal/pattern portion of the in-memory data base. If you assume that the pattern in c[ ] consists of a single element '1' and that the first animal/pattern in the in-memory data base is DOG 10011000110101, then on the first pass of the outside for loop, and on the first pass of the nested for loop, DOG will be written to fname[ ].

However, the for loop must continue to cycle until its exit clause terminates the looping. At this point, control returns to the outside for loop which will allow the second element of the user pattern to be input by the user. Why does this inner loop continue to cycle through the names of all animals in the data base (and the patterns that accompany them) when the user's pattern has not even been completed yet?

The answer is simple and relates directly to speed and efficiency. The nested for loop checks to see if there are any other animals whose pattern combination could possible match the portion of the user's pattern input to this point. If you assume the user's pattern consists of only one element, '1', and that the first pattern element in DOG is also '1', then if all of the other animal patterns in the data base begin with '0', we know they don't apply. It cannot be any of these other animals, so DOG is the only one left to consider. The user may not have a dog in mind at this point. If this is so, then the user's animal is not contained in the data base, but within the expert's "experience", DOG is the only answer to output.

On the other hand, if the looping of the inner for loop turns up another pattern that begins with a '1' (in this discussion), variable i is incremented to 2 which triggers the statements controlled under else. Here, variable i is reassigned a value of 0 zero, and a break statement is executed. This returns control to the outside for loop and another pattern element can be input by the user and the comparison operation can begin anew. When a second possible match was discovered by the nested for loop, an exit to the outer loop occurred, because the program "realizes" that there is more than 1 possibility. There is not yet enough information to decide on a logical outcome.

On the second pass of the outside for loop, the second pattern element is input by the user in response to one of the data base questions.

Let's assume this element is '0'. Now the user pattern is "10". The inner for loop is entered again and this time the "10 pattern is compared with the first two elements of the first pattern in the animal/pattern data base. If there is no match, then the loop continues to cycle until one is found. Again, the animal associated with this pattern is copied to fname[ ] and the rest of the animal/pattern list is checked for the possibility of another pattern that also matches to this point. If there is another possibility, as before, variable i would be incremented to 2 and the outside for loop would bring in yet another user pattern element. Then, a comparison of three pattern elements would ensue.

Remember, when variable i is equal to 1, this means that the incomplete user pattern has been matched to this point and a "suspect" animal is on-board in fname[ ]. If variable i is incremented to 2, this means that there are other possibilities and a determination cannot be made. If, however, variable i is equal to 1 and the inner for loop steps all the way through the entire animal/pattern data base without finding another possible match, the inner loop is exited and an if statement checks for a value of 1 in variable i. If this is the case, the break statement exits the outer for loop and the animal name is provided.

However, if all of the questions are asked of the user, and all of the animals and data base patterns are searched with no match, fname[ ] will still be equal to null and this condition is detected by another if statement which causes the "Don't Know" prompt to appear. If this is not the case (i.e. fname[ ] != '\0'), then the animal name appears.

Each time a single element match is found, an animal name is written to fname[ ]. Even if all pattern elements do not match exactly, an inference is made, based upon the most number of matches. This means that the user can make a few mistakes in answering questions and have a reasonable likelihood of still obtaining an accurate answer. In other words, this program begins to make "guesses" as to which animal it might be, based upon the first question answered by the user. As more and more questions are answered, the program generally becomes surer and surer of a correct answer. In some cases, it may be necessary to ask only two or three questions (out of potentially hundreds) to arrive at a correct answer.

It should be understood that, while this program example is targeted toward the rather elementary purpose of identifying animals based upon user responses to questions, it is by no means limited to such exercises. Hopefully, you can readily see how such a system could be used to serve for any type of subject area. It could be used to, for instance, troubleshoot electronic devices. An expert system in this area would substitute questions about animals for questions about circuits. During the data base building phase of its operation, the learning sequence might look like this:

```
RESULT:SHORT__CIRCUIT__ACROSS__POWER LINE
Question: DOES THE LINE FUSE BLOW
IMMEDIATELY UPON CIRCUIT ACTIVATION
RESULT:AC__HUM
Question: DO THE FILTER CAPACITORS/CHOKE
CHECK OUT AS OPERATIONAL
```

And this system could also be used in debugging C language programs as in:

RESULT: MEMORYOVERWRITE

Question: Does the program work perfectly on some occasions, then suddenly crash on others

RESULT: UNINITIALIZEDVARIABLES

Question: Does the mathematical portion of your program output unusual results that tend to be different during each program run

And this can continue ad infinitum.

The following list shows a printout of an animal data base and the corresponding patterns made with the previous programs:

```
MAN      100000000000000100000000
HORSE    110000000000000000000000
CAT      101000000000000000000000
DOG      100100000000000000000000
FROG     000010000000000000000000
SNAKE    000001000000000000000000
ELEPHANT 110000100000000000000000
CAMEL    110000010000000000000000
WHALE    100000001000000000000000
SHRIMP   000000000100000000000000
EAGLE    000000000010000000000000
LOBSTER  000000000101000000000000
CRAB     000000000100100000000000
COW      100000000000100000001000
RABBIT   100000000000010000000000
ROBIN    000000000000001000000000
MONKEY   100000000000000100000000
SPIDER   000000000000000010000000
BEE      000000000000000001000000
TURTLE   000000000000000000100000
PORCUPINE 100000000000000000010000
DEER     100000000000000000001000
TURKEY   000000000000000000000100
GOAT     100000000000100000001010
SHEEP    100000000000100000001001
```

Naturally, this animal/pattern data is useless without the questions that were used to arrive at the patterns. The pattern file contents are shown in the following list:

    DOES THIS ANIMAL NURSE ITS YOUNG WITH MILK
    DO PEOPLE RIDE ON IT
    DOES IT PURR
    IS IT A DOMESTIC PET THAT BARKS
    DOES IT BEGIN LIFE AS A TADPOLE
    IS THIS AN ANIMAL WITH NO ARMS OR LEGS THAT SLITHERS
    IS THIS A VERY LARGE ANIMAL WITH A TRUNK
    IS THIS A DESERT ANIMAL WITH A SINGLE OR DOUBLE HUMP
    IS THIS A LARGE SEA CREATURE THAT BREATHES AIR
    IS THIS A SMALL SEA CREATURE THAT IS NOT A FISH AND IS EATEN BY HUMANS
    IS THIS ANIMAL A LARGE BIRD THAT IS A NATIONAL SYMBOL
    IS THIS AN EDIBLE SEA CREATURE NOTED FOR THE MEAT IN ITS TAIL AND CLAWS
    IS THIS AN EDIBLE SEA CREATURE THAT WALKS SIDEWAYS
    IS THIS A FARM ANIMAL THAT PROVIDES MILK FOR HUMAN CONSUMPTION
    IS THIS A FAST LONG-EARED ANIMAL THAT IS VERY PROLIFIC
    IS THIS A BIRD WITH A BRIGHT RED BREAST
    IS THIS ANIMAL SOMEWHAT HUMAN IN APPEARANCE
    DOES IT HAVE EIGHT LEGS AND SOMETIMES BITES
    IS THIS AN INSECT THAT PRODUCES HONEY
    IS THIS A SLOW-MOVING REPTILE WITH A SHELL
    DOES THIS ANIMAL HAVE QUILLS FOR DEFENSE
    IS THIS AN ANTLERED ANIMAL VERY COMMON IN MANY COUNTRIES
    IS THIS A BIRD THAT IS OFTEN SERVED ON SPECIAL HOLIDAYS
    IS THE MALE OF THE SPECIES CALLED A BILLY
    ARE FEMALES OF THE SPECIES CALLED EWES

Naturally, inputting this information and "teaching" the program to utilize the data can be a long process, although the mini data base above was input in about ten minutes. When data bases get to be much larger, on the order of thousands of items, then the inputting/teaching procedure can take weeks or even months. Such are the requirements of developing a good, commercial quality data base for expert system applications.

AN EXPERT SYSTEM

The program in FIG. 6-9 is a combined and slightly altered version of the two (one for storing data—the other for loading and using it) just discussed. It is not slanted toward one specific type of expert system as was the case with the last two, and it can be used immediately to incorporate your own expert data base.

This program was made from the previous two and incorporates a few subtle but excellent improvements. Because this program was pieced together form the other two, two goto statements are used to branch to the various program portions. The use of goto in C language programs is generally frowned upon, because it tends to destroy structure. I am certainly in agreement with this idea. However, in this case, I don't believe the structure is adversely affected, as I am dealing with separate program blocks that have been linked together. In any event, I believe the separation of the blocks will provide a clearer idea to the reader of the separate operations that are taking place. At the same time, I will reaffirm that the use of goto in C language programs should be avoided whenever possible or practical to do so. Much better structure and understanding can (usually) be had by adhering to this practice.

In this program, item[ ] is the array that is used to hold the result and its pattern. Array quesm[ ] contains the questions from which the patterns are established. Upon execution, a prompt asks whether the user wishes to use the expert system or build a data base. Regardless of which choice is made, the familiar routine of "nulling out" each element in the two data arrays takes place from within the for loop.

Next, an if statement tests the results of the prompt. If x = = '1', then the user is seeking access to the expert system. This causes a program branch to the label named qrp:, however we will assume for now that the user wishes to add to or build a data base.

When a data base is to be built, it is first necessary to load the contents of the current data base files on disk. If data base files already exist, these will be added to. Therefore, if you wish to replace the current data base with a new one, it is first necessary to erase both data base files before invoking this program. Let's assume that the data base is being built for the first time, and there are no data base files on disk.

Within an if statement construct, an attempt is made to open the two data base files for read-only operations. If these files don't exist (and in this portion of the discussion, they do not), a NULL is returned and the execution chain skips down to the assignment line:

```
count = 0;
```

Fig. 6-9. It loads and stores its database.

```
#include <stdio.h>
main()
{
    char item[100][100];
    char quesm[100][80], name[30], code[200], fname[30];
    char *p, *f, question[100], result[40], c[100], d[10];
    int i, k, q, x, y, z, count;
    FILE *fp, *fpp;

    while (k != '1' && k != '2') {
        puts("Type 1 to use Expert System -- 2 to add to (build) data base");
        k = toupper(getch());
    }

    for (x = 0; x < 100; ++x)
        quesm[x][0] = item[x][0] = '\0';

    if (k == '1')
        goto qrp;

    if ((fp = fopen("fibase.dat", "r")) != NULL && (fpp = fopen("quesfile", "r")) != NULL) {
        x = 0;
        while ((fgets(item[x], 100, fp)) != NULL) {
            item[x][strlen(item[x]) - 1] = '\0';
            ++x;
        }

        x = 0;
        while ((fgets(quesm[x], 100, fpp)) != NULL) {
            quesm[x][strlen(quesm[x]) - 1] = '\0';
            ++x;

        }

        fclose(fp);
        fclose(fpp);

    }

    count = 0;
    for (x = 0; ; ++x) {
        if (quesm[x][0] != '\0') {
            ++count;
            continue;
        }

        printf("Name an item that is not a part of the data base: ");
        gets(result);
        strupr(result);
        y = 0;
        while (item[y][0] != '\0') {
            if (item[y][0] != '\"' && strncmp(item[y], result,
```

(Fig. 6-9 cont.)

```c
              strlen (result)) == 0) {
                        printf("Item already exists in data base\n");
                        y = -1;
                             break;
                   }
                   y++;
              }
              if (y == -1)
                   continue;

              strcpy(item[y], result);

              printf("Type a question that pertains to the %s\n", result);
              gets(question);
              strupr(question);

              y = 0;
              while (strcmp(item[y], result) != 0) {
                   printf("\n\n%s:\n%s(Y/N)? ", item[y], question);
                   z = toupper(getch());
                   if (z == 'Y')
                        z = 1;
                   else if (z == 'N')
                        z = 0;
                   else if (z == 'I')
                        z = 3;
                   else {
                        --y;
                        continue;
                   }

                   sprintf(c, "%d", z);
                   strcat(item[y++], c);
              }

              i = y;
              strcpy(quesm[y], question);
              strcat(item[y], " ");
              for (y = 0; quesm[y][0] != '\0'; ++y) {
                   printf("\n\n%s:\n%s(Y/N)", result, quesm[y]);
                   z = toupper(getch());
                   if (z == 'Y')
                        z = 1;
                   else if (z == 'N')
                        z = 0;
                   else if (z == 'I')
                        z = 3;
                    else {
                        --y;
                        continue;
                   }
                   sprintf(c, "%d", z);
                   strcat(item[i], c);
              }
```

(Fig. 6-9 cont.)

```c
                printf("\n\nContinue(Y/N)?");
                z = toupper(getch());
                puts(" ");
                if (z == 'N') {
                        if ((fp = fopen("fibase.dat", "a")) == NULL) {
                                puts("Can't Write fibase.dat");
                                exit(0);
                        }
                        if ((fpp = fopen("quesfile", "a")) == NULL) {
                                puts("Can't write quesfile");
                                exit(0);
                        }
                        for (x = count; item[x][0] != '\0'; ++x) {
                                fprintf(fp, "%s\n", item[x]);
                                fprintf(fpp, "%s\n", quesm[x]);
                        }
                        fclose(fp);
                        fclose(fpp);

                        break;
                }
        }
qrp:
        puts("Do you wish to use the Expert System(Y/N)?\n");
        x = toupper(getch());
        if (x == 'N')
                exit(0);
        else {
                if ((fp = fopen("fibase.dat", "r")) == NULL) {
                        puts("Cannot open data base file");
                        exit(0);
                }
                if ((fpp = fopen("quesfile", "r")) == NULL) {
                        puts("Cannot open data base question file");
                        exit(0);
                }

                x = 0;
                while ((fgets(item[x], 100, fp)) != NULL) {
                        item[x][strlen(item[x]) - 1] = '\0';
                        ++x;
                }

                fclose(fp);

                x = 0;
                while ((fgets(quesm[x], 100, fpp)) != NULL) {
                        quesm[x][strlen(quesm[x]) - 1] = '\0';
                        ++x;

                }

                fclose(fpp);
        }
```

(Fig. 6-9 cont.)

```
qrd:
    printf("\n\n\n\n\n\n\n\n\n\n\n\n\n\n\n\n");

    printf("                         EXPERT SYSTEM\n\n");

    c[0] = d[0] = name [0] = fname[0] = code[0] = '\0';
    i = q = x = y = 0;
    for (x = 0; quesm[x][0] != '\0'; ++x) {
        printf("\n\n%s(Y/N)? ", quesm[x]);
        y = toupper(getch());
        if (y == 'Y')
            y = 1;
        else if (y == 'N')
            y = 0;
        else {
            --x;
            continue;
        }

        sprintf(d, "%d", y);
        strcat(c, d);

        i = 0;
        for (z = q; item[z][0] != '\0'; ++z) {
            sscanf(item[z], "%s %s", name, code);
            if (strncmp(c, code, strlen(c)) == 0) {
                ++i;
                if (i == 1) {
                    strcpy(fname, name);
                }
                else if (i == 2) {
                    i = 0;
                    break;
                }
            }

        }
        if (i == 1)
            break;
    }
    printf("\n\n\nI believe you have described %s.\n", fname);
    printf("\n\nDo you wish to continue(Y/N)?%c\n", 7);

    x = toupper(getch());
    if (x == 'Y')
        goto qrd;

}
```

The operation of the skipped over program segment will be explored a bit later.

As with the case with the previous program, an endless for loop is entered and, immediately, an if statement checks for the end of the data base array question list. This is evidenced by the first element in the array line being equal to '\0'. Because there are no questions at all in this array, the first line yields the '\0'. As before, a printf( ) function is used to prompt the user to input data base items. This item is temporarily copied to result[ ] and a while loop is entered.

Here is where one of the changes occurs. A new item has been added to the if statement line that tests for the repetition of a data base item. With this addition, if the first character of the item in the data base is the quotation mark (usually referred to as "double quotes" in C language), the conditional test ends right there. This means that more than one result beginning with double quotes (") is permitted, whereas only one of any other type of result is allowed. The reason for this change will be discussed shortly. Once the string in result[ ] has been tested and permitted to pass, the same routine that was discussed for the previous loading program is executed. The user is asked to input a question that pertains to the result. This question is then applied to every other item in the data base, and the user responds with the usual 'Y' or 'N'.

However, the user is also permitted another, valid option. This is arbitrarily chosen as 'I', which stands for "Ignore". As before, the 'Y' and the 'N' equate to numeric values of 1 and 0, respectively, An input of 'I' equates to numeric 3, a value that is also arbitrarily chosen. The value of an 'I' response must be different from the other possible responses. That is the main concern. The reason for the addition of the 'I' response hinges to the previous check for an opening double quotes character.

As each question is answered by the expert user, a pattern is built an element at a time in item[ ]. When all items and patterns have been added by the expert user, an 'N' response to the "Continue?" prompt will cause this portion of the program to be exited.

Now, it is necessary to "dump" the information in the data base arrays into the data base disk files. As before, the disk files are opened for "append" operations. Because no files currently exist at this point in the discussion, the append operation automatically becomes a write operation wherein files are created and written to from their beginning.

At this point the user is granted access to the expert system which, if utilized, will reload the file information just saved. This portion of the program is identical to the very last program discussed.

Return to the beginning of the program. Assume that a data base has been input and saved to disk. Assume also that you wish to add information to the disk data base files already established. Again, the user would respond with a '2' to the access prompt.

This time, however, the if statement test of opening two disk files is successful, and these files are open for read-only operations. The fgets( )

function is called several times to load this file information into the proper arrays.

When this operation is completed, the files are closed and the endless for loop is entered. Now, the if statement detects the presence of string data in the question array (more accurately, it doesn't detect a null character) and executes the continue statement. This causes the endless for loop to cycle again, incrementing the value of variable x. The next array position in quesm[ ] is checked and continue is executed again. This process occurs over and over until the value of x has been advanced to a point that corresponds to the first empty array position in quesm[ ]. This is the point at which new data base information may be added without overwriting that which had been input and saved previously.

Prior to each execution of the continue statement, variable count is incremented by 1. This variable keeps tract of the array position where the start of the new information write begins.

At the end of the loading/teaching segment, the array information is again written to disk file. Here the files are open for an append, so any information written to these files will be written to the end of what is already there. The files write operation is made using two fprintf( ) functions from within a for loop. This loop initially assigns loop variable, x, a value equal to count. This means that only the new information will be appended to the disk file.

You might wonder why this is done, when all of the information already contained in these files has been loaded into the arrays before adding the new information. Why not just rewrite the file using all of the information in the arrays? After all, the same information would be transferred. This is true if you assume that the write of the newly updated array is successful. However, this could lead to the destruction of an entire data base!

Each time you write a file ("w" mode in C language), any other file by the same name is overwritten. Suppose you have loaded the information from fidbase.dat into memory. We add information to it, and then write the entire array contents backs to fibase.dat. In the process, the original fibase file is destroyed and overwritten by the newly updated version. No problem. But what if a machine power, or write failure takes place midway through this operation. The original contents of the file could be erased. However, with an append operation, you are only adding to what is already there. There is far less chance of catastrophic file loss when you update a file by appending information then if you try to completely overwrite it with new data.

Now, what about double quotes character? This is added as a "wild card," so to speak. The double quotes option allows users to input a question without a subsequent result. Remember, each question is applied to each and every result in the data base. However, previous program examples made no provision for asking two or more questions about a particular object, because duplicate results were disallowed.

Now, if you want ask more than one question about an item, simply type the item name and then input the first question. When the teaching segment is completed, you will be asked for another item. Here, you may input the double quotes. You will be asked to supply a question that pertains to (''). Simply type any question you want. The program will then ask this question of all items in the data base. When it asks if this question applied to (''), respond with 'I'. This causes a pattern of 3's to be established for all double quote entries. Such a pattern will never match an actual result that will have a pattern of 1s and 0s.

Remember, the question that accompanies a result does not necessarily have to apply positively to that result. Remember also that any question applies as much to all other results as it does to the one that prompted the question in the first place. The ability to ask multiple questions, without having to come up with a valid and different result for each one, is a very valuable addition to this form of expert system.

SUMMARY

In this chapter, some of the basics of expert system design have been discussed in detail, and programming methods where shown to implement them. Some types of simple experts have used a "brute force " method incorporating if statement constructs that address the limited number of results. Others have used a mathematical calculation based on Poisson's formula, and still others have depended upon a complex pattern match to achieve logical outputs or to make the proper inferences. Another type has assigned fractional values to conditions, seeking to establish unity in order to return a result. And there are other methods which have been tried, others that are being tried and still others that will be tried.

The C language lends itself well to all of these methods. Its speed of execution makes it especially applicable when compared with several other languages. C has the capability of quickly sorting through the very long lists of objects that are normally associated with AI programs and knowledge-based expert systems. By understanding the beginning concepts of these practices, you should be able to move onward and upward with your personal learning experiences in the field of artificial intelligence programming for expert systems using the C programming language.

Appendix A
Listings for Chapter 3

Fig. A-1. The binomial( ) function returns a probability calculation.

```
double binomial(n, p, q)
double p, q;
int n;
{
    int x, y;
    double t, mu, pow();

    if (n <= 0)         /* Illegal argument   return error (-1) */
        return(-1);

    if (n == 1);  /* First binomial term */
        return(pow(p, (double) n));  /* Return first term */
    if (n == 2)
        return(n * pow(p, n - 1.0) * q); /* Second binomial term */

    y = 1;
    mu = (n * (n - 1));
    for (x = 2; x < n; ++x) { /* Loop through n - 1 for correct term */
        t = (mu / (x * y)) * pow(p, n - (double) x) * pow(q, (double) x);
        y *= x;      /*         y = y * x        */
        mu *= (n - x);    /*       mu = mu * (n - x)      */
    }

    return(t);  /* Return value */

}
```

Fig. A-2. Making use of the binomial function.

```c
/* Making use of the binomial function */
main()
{
    double p, q, binomial();
    int n;

    printf("Type the value of p, q, and n\n");
    scanf("%lf %lf %d", &p, &q, &n); /* Scan keyboard for values */

    printf("%lf\n", binomial(n, p, q)); /* Call function with values */

}
```

Fig. A-3. This binomial( ) returns each term.

```c
/* Write binomial values to double array pointed to by *z */
binomial(z, n, p, q)
double p, q, *z;
int n;
{
    int x, y;
    double mu, pow();

    if (n <= 0)   /* Illegal value */
        return(-1);    /* Retun an error code */

    *z++ = pow(p, (double) n); /* First binomial term   increment *z */
    if (n == 1) {
        *z++ = pow(q, (double) n); /* Second term   increment *z */
        return(0);   /* Return success */
    }

    *z++ = n * pow(p, n - 1.0) * q;   /* Continue   increment *z */
    if (n == 2) {   /* Number == 2 */
        *z++ = pow(q, (double) n); /* *z == q raised to 2 */
        return(0); /* Success */
    }

    y = 1;
    mu = (n * (n - 1));

    for (x = 2; x < n; ++x) {   /* Loop through n -1 */
        *z++ = (mu / (x * y)) * pow(p, n-(double) x) * pow(q, (double) x);
        y *= x;
        mu *= (n - x);
    }

    *z = pow(q, (double) n); /* Write z */

    return(0);  /* Return success */

}
```

Fig. A-4. Here is a typical calling routine.

```
/* Calling binomial() */
main()
{
    double p, q, *b, ar[20];
    int n, x;

    b = ar;  /* b is a pointer that contains the address of ar[] */

    printf("Type p, q, n\n");
    scanf("%lf %lf %d", &p, &q, &n); /* Get argument values */

    binomial(b, n, p, q); /* Call binomial() */

    for (x = 0; x <= n; ++x)
        printf("%lf\n", ar[x]); /* Display each result */
}
```

Fig. A-5. Here is an example of global variable usage.

```
double ar[20];   /* ar[] is a global array */
main()
{
    double p, q;
    int n, x;

    b = ar;

    printf("Type p, q, n\n");
    scanf("%lf %lf %d", &p, &q, &n);

    binomial(n, p, q);

    for (x = 0; x <= n; ++x)
        printf("%lf\n", ar[x]);

}
binomial(n, p, q)
double p, q;
int n;
{
    int x, y;
    double mu, pow();

    if (n <= 0)
        return(-1);
    /* Same as before, but global array is used instead of array pointer */
    ar[0] = pow(p, (double) n);
```

(Fig. A-5 cont.)

```
        if (n == 1) {
             ar[1] = pow(q, (double) n);
             return(0);
        }

        ar[1] = n * pow(p, n - 1.0) * q;
        if (n == 2) {
             ar[2] = pow(q, (double) n);
             return(0);
        }

        y = 1;
        mu = (n * (n - 1));

        for (x = 2; x < n; ++x) {
             ar[x] = (mu / (x * y)) * pow(p, n-(double) x) * pow(q, (double) x
             y *= x;
             mu *= (n - x);
        }

        ar[x] = pow(q, (double) n);

        return(0);

}
```

Fig. A-6. This is poisson( ), a modification of binomial( ).

```
/* Poisson's Probability Formula */
poisson(z, i)
double *z;    /*    *z points to a double array */
int i;              /* Occurrences */
{
        int x, y;
        double e, m, em, pow();

        e = 2.7183; /* Base of Napierian logarithms */
        m = i;
        em = pow(e, -m);   /* First term */

        if (m <= 0)
             return(-1);   /* Illegal value in i */

        *z++ = em;      /* First term return */
        *z++ = m * em;  /* Second term return */

        y = 1;
        for (x = 2; x < 10; ++x) {  /* Loop through remaining terms */
             *z++ = (pow(m, (double) x) / (x * y)) * em; /* x term */
             y *= x;

        }

        return(0); /* Return to calling program */

}
```

Fig. A-7. A typical program that calls poisson( ).

```
/* Calling poisson() */
main()
{
      double *b, ar[10];
      int i, x;

      b = ar;    /* b points to ar[] */

      printf("How many times has this event occurred in the past?\n");
      scanf("%d", &i);   /* Get integer response to i */

      poisson(b, i);   /* b == aray to write results to */

      for (x = 0; x < 8; ++x)    /* Display results */
            printf("Chance of reoccurrence %d times is %lf\n", x, b[x - 1]);

}
```

Appendix B
Listings for Chapter 4

Fig. B-1. "Guess My Number!"

```c
/* User guesses computer's number */
main()
{
    int guess, actual, x;
    double y;

    guess = -1;     /* initialize guess to -1 */

    puts("Type any positive integer");  /* random seed prompt */
    scanf("%d", &x);      /* get response to x */

    srand(x);            /* Reseed random number generator */
    x = y = (double) rand() / rand(); /* Get random value */
    y -= x;    /* Remove any whole number value */
    actual = y * 100 + 1;    /* actual = random integer 1 to 100 */
    x = 0;

    puts("I am thinking of a whole number of from 1 to 100");
    puts("Input your guess");

    while (guess != actual) {  /* while guess is not correct */
        scanf("%d", &guess);   /* get a guess from the keyboard */
```

(Fig. B-1 cont.)

```
        /* determination rule */

            if (guess < actual)    /* guess is less than actual */
                puts("Too Low. Guess again"); /* too low prompt */
            if (guess > actual)    /* guess is more than actual */
                puts("Too high. Guess Again"); /* too high prompt */
            ++x;  /* increment x  x = number of guesses */
    }

        /* loop is exited because guess = actual */
        /* print prompt */

        Printf("That's It!!! You got it in %d guesses.\n", x);

}
```

Fig. B-2. This program plays "Guess My Number!"

```
/* Computer guesses user's number */

main()
{
        int low, high, guess, count;
        char c;

        puts("Think of a whole number of from 1 to 100");
        puts("When you have a number in mind, press <ENTER>");
        scanf("%c", &c); /* halt execution until <enter> 

        count = 0; /* count = number of guesses */
        low = 0;   /* lower limit */
        high = 100; /* upper limit */
        guess = high / 2; /* first best guess */

        while (low != high - 1) {  /* while guess is incorrect */
              printf("Is your number less than %d (Y/N)\n", guess);
              c = getch(); /* get user directions (high, low) */
              if (c == 'y' || c == 'Y') /* check for yes answer */
                    high = guess; /* upper range now equals guess */
              else
                    low = guess; /* guess is low, so lower limit is reset */

              guess = high - ((high - low) / 2); /* next best guess */
              ++count; /* increment count which holds number of guesses */
        }

        /* correct number has been determined */

        printf("Your number is %d. It took me %d guesses.\n", low, count);

}
```

Fig. B-3. This program plays itself at "Guess My Number!"

```c
/* Computer plays number games with itself */
int guess, high, low; /* external variables */
main()
{
    int actual, count, x;
    double y;
    char c;

    printf("Press any key to reseed generator.\n");
    c = getch();  /* get random number generator seed value */
    srand(c);

    /* random number generator routine */
    count = 0;
    x = y = (double) rand() / rand();
    y -= x;
    actual = y * 100 + 1;   /* random number to be guesses */

    guess = 50;  /* first best guess */
    high = 100;  /* high limit */
    low = 0;     /* low limit */

    while (guess != actual) {  /* while number is not guesses */
        printf("MY GUESS IS %d\n\n", guess);/* print guess */
        if (guess < actual) {    /* if guess low */
            printf("Too Low--Try Again\n\n"); /* too low prompt */
            newguess("low");  /* call newguess */
        }
        else {                   /* guess too high */
            printf("Too High--Try Again\n\n");  /* too high prompt */
            newguess("high"); /* call newguess */
        }
        ++count;  /* keep track og guesses */
    }

    /* correct guess has been determined */

    printf("MY GUESS IS %d\n\n", guess);
    printf("That is correct. It took you %d guesses.\n", ++count);

}
/* arrive at a best new guess based upon last old guess */
newguess(a)
char a[];  /* "high" or "low" indicator */
{
    if (strcmp(a, "low") == 0)  /* if last guess is low */
        low = guess;      /* variable low = last guess */
    else                  /* last guess is high */
        high = guess;     /* upper limit is assigned value of last guess */
```

(Fig. B-3 cont.)

```
        guess = high - ((high - low) / 2); /* new best guess judgement rile */

        /* Note: variables low, high, and guess are external (global) */
        /* and are known to all program elements including the newguess */
        /* function. Therefore, it is not necessary to return the value */
        /* of guess to the calling program. */
}
```

Fig. B-4. Return a random integer from 1 to 6.

```
    rand6()   /* Return a random integer from 1 to 6 */
    {
        double a;
        int x;

        srand(seed);  /* seed is a global variable */

        /* divide rand() by itself to arrive at pseudo random number */
        /* a = the actual return from this operation (floating point) */
        /* x = the integer value of this operation */

        x = a = (double) rand() / rand();
        a -= x; /* by subtracting the integer from the whole value */
                /* the fractional portion of the original return */
                /* is extracted. This is the needed random value */

        x = a * 6 + 1; /* a is less than 1, therefore a * 6 is */
                       /* always less than 6. By adding one, the */
                       /* highest possible integer value is 6 */
                       /* Likewise, a is more than zero but can */
                       /* be less than 1, so a * 6 might equate */
                       /* to integer 0. a * 6 + 1 will always be */
                       /* equal to or more than 1 */

        return(x);  /* Return random integer of from 1 to 6 */

    }
```

Fig. B-5. Return a pseudo-random number.

```
    main()
    {
        int r[6], x, y;

        r[0] = r[1] = r[2] = r[3] = r[4] = r[5] = 0;

        printf("input an integer value of from 1 to 30000\n");
        scanf("%d", &x);   /* get seed value to x */
```

(Fig. B-5 cont.)

```
        srand(x);  /* seed random number generator */

        for (y = 1; y <= 15000; ++y) {   /* Do 15000 iterations */
                x = rand6();    /* call random number routine */
                switch(x) {     /* test for each value of 1 to 6 */
                        case 1:         /* does x == 1 */
                                ++r[0]; /* if sp, increment r[0] */
                                break;  /* break out of switch tree */
                        case 2:         /* does x == 2 */
                                ++r[1]; /* if so, increment r[1] */
                                break;  /* etc. */
                        case 3:         /* etc. */
                                ++r[2];
                                break;
                        case 4:
                                ++r[3];
                                break;
                        case 5:
                                ++r[4];
                                break;
                        case 6:
                                ++r[5];

        }
/* Display results as random values are recorded */

        printf("%-8d%-8d%-8d%-8d%-8d%-8d%-8d\n", y, r[0], r[1], r[2],
r[3], r[4], r[5]);
        }

}
/* Source code for rand6() goes here */
```

Appendix C
Listings for Chapter 5

Fig. C-1. The contents of a header file.

```
/* Header File for memory file operations */
            struct vfile {         /* declare structure */
                char *fiptr;       /* file pointer */
                long vfiloc;       /* location in file */
            } VFIL[20];            /* An array of structures (20) */

            #define VFILE struct vfile   /* Give it an easy name */

            VFILE *v[20];          /* v[] is a pointer to the struct */
            char *finame[20];      /* an array of char pointers */
            int fino = 0;          /* beginning file number is 0 */
```

Fig. C-2. vopen( ) opens a memory file.

```
/* Open a memory file */

VFILE *vopen(a, b, bytes)    /* returns pointer of type VFILE */
char *a, *b;     /*a = memory file name -- b = type of file */
unsigned bytes; /* bytes = size of file */
{
```

(Fig. C-2 cont.)

```c
        char *calloc(), malloc();
        int i;

        /* find out what type of file, i.e. read or append
        if (strcmp(b, "r") == 0 || strcmp(b, "a") == 0) {
            for (i = 0; i < fino; ++i)
                if (strcmp(a, finame[i]) == 0) {
                    v[i] = &VFIL[i];    /* v[i] points to struct */
                    if (strcmp(b, "r") == 0)
                        v[i]->vfiloc = 0L;  /* start at position zero */
                    else
                        v[i]->vfiloc = (long) strlen(v[i]->fiptr);

                    return(v[i]);  /* return memory file pointer */
                }
        }
        /* check for write file */
        else if (strcmp(b, "w") == 0) {
            v[fino] = &VFIL[fino]; /* v[fino] points to struct */
            v[fino]->vfiloc = 0L;  /* begin at 0 (long int) */

            /* Make sure there is enough memory available */
            if ((v[fino]->fiptr = calloc(bytes, 1)) == NULL) {
                puts("Out of Memory");  /* if not, print prompt and */
                exit(0);                /* exit program */
            }

            strcpy(finame[fino] = malloc(20), a); /* record file name */
            fino++;              /* advance file number for next file */
            return(v[fino - 1]);
        }
        else
            return(NULL);   /* error in call, return NULL */
}
```

Fig. C-3. vputs( ) writes to or reads from a memory file.

```c
/* write a string to a memory file */

vputs(a, ptr)
char *a;       /* points to string */
VFILE *ptr;    /* points to memory file */
{

    /* write string a character at a time */
    /* increment file pointer by one after each write */

    while (*(ptr->fiptr + ptr->vfiloc) = *a++)
        ++ptr->vfiloc;

}
```

Fig. C-4. vgets( ) reads a string of characters from a file.

```
/* read a character string from a memory file */

vgets(a, x, ptr)
char *a;    /* must be large enough to hold x characters */
int x;      /* maximum number of characters to read */
VFILE *ptr; /* points to open memory file */
{
    int ct = 0;

    if (*(ptr->fiptr + ptr->vfiloc) == '\0')
        return(NULL);  /* empty file or not open */

    /* write characters to *a one at a time */
    /* until x characters are transferred or a newline(\n) is read */

    while ((*a++ = *(ptr->fiptr + ptr->vfiloc)) != '\n' && ct < x) {
            ++ptr->vfiloc;  /* advance pointer to file location by one */
            ++ct;           /* number of characters read */
    }

    ++ptr->vfiloc; /* advance file location by one */
    *a = '\0';     /* terminate characters with \0 to make a string */

    return(1);     /* a return of 1 indicates success */

}
```

Fig. C-5. vwind( ) is the memory file equivalent of C'w rewind( ).

```
vwind(ptr)    /* return pointer to 0 position */
VFILE *ptr;   /* points to open file */
{
    ptr->vfiloc = 0L; /* new location = 0L */

}
```

Fig. C-6. vtell( ) reveals the current file offset.

```
long vtell(ptr)   /* returns long int value */
VFILE *ptr;       /* points to open file */
{
    /* return value of file location */

    return (ptr->vfiloc);

 }
```

Fig. C-7. vseek( ) moves the file pointer offset.

```c
/* seek to new file position */

vseek(ptr, off, mode)
VFILE *ptr;  /* points to open memory file */
long off;    /* offset value is a long integer */
int mode;  /* mode = 0, offset from beginning */
           /* mode = 1, offset from current file position */
{
    if (mode < 0 || mode > 1)    /* bas mode argument */
        return(-1);              /* therefore, return error */
    else if (mode == 0)      /* offset from file beginning */
        ptr->filoc;       /* set file location pointer to absolute value */
    else if (mode == 1) /* offset from current file position */
        ptr->vfiloc += off; /* add value to current position */

    return(0)           /* return success */

}
```

Fig. C-8. vclose( ) maintains conventional points of reference.

```c
/* close memory file */

vclose(ptr)
VFILE *ptr;  /* pointer to open file */
{
    *ptr = '\0';  /* assign pointer NULL value */

}
```

Fig. C-9. vputc( ) writes single characters to a file.

```c
/* write a single character to a memory file */

vputc(a, ptr)
int a;        /* a = character */
VFILE *ptr;  /* points to open file */
{
    /* assign file character in a to file */

    *(ptr->fiptr + ptr->vfiloc) = a;
    ++ptr->vfiloc; /* step to next file location */

}
```

Fig. C-10. vgetc( ) retrieves single characters from a file.

```
/* get a single character from memory file */

vgetc(ptr)
VFILE *ptr;   /* points to open file */
{
      int a;

      /* a = character from file */
      a = *(ptr->fiptr + ptr->vfiloc);

      ++ptr->vfiloc;  /* advance pointer to next character *

      if (a == '\0')  /* check for end of file */
           return(-1);/* if so, return EOF */
      else
           return(a); /* else return character */

}
```

Fig. C-11. vlink( ) clears a reserved block of memory.

```
/* erase file from memory */

vlink(a)
char *a; /* a points to file name */
{
      int i;
      /* step through list of file names */
      for (i = 0; i <= fino; ++i)
           /* if name is found */
           if (strcmp(a, finame[i]) == 0) {
                free(v[i]->fiptr); /*free pointer */
                free(finame[i]); /* free name array */
                break;
           }
}
```

Listings for Chapter 5

Appendix D
Listings for Chapter 6

Fig. D-1. This expert system determines whether an animal is a mammal or not

```
main()
{
    int x;

    puts("Does this animal nurse its young(Y/N)?");
    scanf("%d", &x);    /* get input from keyboard */

     /* determination rule */

    if (x == 'Y')
        puts("The animal is a mammal.");
    else
        puts("The animal is not a mammal.");

}
```

Fig. D-2. This program allows for a "don't know" answer.

```
/* D = Don't Know */
main()
{
    int x;
```

(Fig. D-2 cont.)

```c
        puts("Does this animal nurse its young(Y/N/D)?");
        scanf("%d", &x);    /* get keyboard input to x */


        /* first determination rule */

        if (x == 'Y')
            puts("This animal is a mammal");
        else if (x == 'N')
            puts("This animal is not a mammal");
        else {        /* first part of rule doesn't apply */
                      /* ask another question */
            puts("Is this a furry, warm-blooded animal(Y/N)?");
            scanf("%d", &x);   /* get keyboard input to x */

            /* second determination rule */
            if (x == 'Y')
                  puts("This animal is probably a mammal");
            if (x == 'N')
                  puts("This animal is probably not a mammal");
        }

}
```

Fig. D-3. This program has a best guess.

```c
main()
{
    int x, ct;
    double y;
    char *q[5];

    /* static array holds (Y/N) answer values */
    static double z[5][2] = {
        { 0.33, -1.0 },
        { -0.75, 0.25 },
        { -0.75, 0.25 },
        { 0.75, -0.75 },
        { 1.0, -1.0 }
    };


    /* array q[] contains questions for which answer values */
    /* have been pre determined in z[][] */

    q[0] = "Does this animal have bones(Y/N/D)?";
    q[1] = "Does this animal fly(Y/N/D)?";
    q[2] = "Does this animal have a bill(Y/N/D)?";
    q[3] = "Does this animal have fur(Y/N/D)?";
    q[4] = "Does this animal nurse its young(Y/N/D)?";

    x = ct = 0;
    y = 0.0;
```

(Fig. D-3 cont.)

```
        printf("EXPERT SYSTEM\n\n");
        printf("    MAMMALS\n\n");

        /* while loop cycles  while answer values are less than */
        /* abs 1 or until all questions have been asked */

        while (y > -1 && y < 1 && ct < 5) {
            printf("%s\n", q[ct]);  /* display question */
            x = toupper(getch());   /* get response in upper case */

            /* this section evaluates answers */
            if (x == 'Y')
                x = 0;  /* first array position */
            else if (x == 'N')
                x = 1;  /* second array position */
            else {          /* don't know response */
                ++ct;   /* keep count of questions asked */
                continue;    /* loop again */
            }
            y += z[ct++][x];   /* answer is Y or N, so increment */
                               /* variable y by value in z[][] */

        }

        /* determination rule */

        if (y >= 1.0)   /* positive value of 1 or greater */
            printf("This animal is a mammal\n");  /* mammal */
        else if (y <= -1)  /* negative value of -1 or less */
            printf("This animal is not a mammal\n"); /* not a mammal */
        else if (y > 0)  /* positive value but less than 1 */
            printf("This animal is probably a mammal\n"); /* prob a mammal */
        else if (y < 0)  /* negative value but more than -1 */
            printf("This animal is probably not a mammal\n");/* prob not mammal */
        else    /* y == 0 */
            printf("Not enough information to decide\n");   /* don't know */

}
```

Fig. D-4. This program has a variable database.

```
#include <stdio.h>
main()
{

    int x, ct;
    double y, z[100][2];
    char q[5][100], ques[80], num1[10], num2[10];
    char res[20][100];
    FILE *fp, *fpp;

    ct = 1;
```

(Fig. D-4 cont.)

```c
        printf("Do you wish to construct a data bank(Y/N)\n");
        if ((x = toupper(getch())) == 'Y') {   /* Build data bank */
            /* Open disk files */
            if ((fp = fopen("xpbase", "w")) == NULL) {
                printf("Can't open data base file%d\n", 7);
                exit(0);
            }
            while(x) {   /* Endless loop */
                printf("Type question #%d\n", ct++);
                gets(ques); /* Write user question to ques[] */
                if (strcmp(ques, "end") == 0) {  /* Check for "end" */
                    fclose(fp); /* END    close file */
                    break;      /* \exit endless loop */
                }
                printf("If answered yes, what is the value?\n");
                gets(num1); /* Value for positive answer */
                printf("If answered no, what is the value?\n");
                gets(num2);/* Value for negative answer */

                Write rules to file */
                fprintf(fp, "%s:%s:\n%s\n", num1, num2, ques);

            }
            fclose(fp);    /* Close file */

            ct = 0;

            /* Open result file */
            if ((fpp = fopen("xpresult", "w")) == NULL) {
                printf("Can't open result file.\n");
                exit(0);
            }
        printf("Type the result of a positive outcome\n");
        gets(res[ct]);   /* Get positive result */
        fprintf(fpp, "%s\n", res[ct++]); /* Write it to file */
        printf("\n\nType the result of a negative outcome.\n");
        gets(res[ct]);   /* Get negative result */
        fprintf(fpp, "%s\n", res[ct++]); /* Write it to file */
        printf("\n\nType the result of a probable positive outcome.\n");
        gets(res[ct]);   /* Get probably positive result */
        fprintf(fpp, "%s\n", res[ct++]); /* Write it */
        printf("\n\nType the result of a probable negative
outcome.\n");
        gets(res[ct]);   /* Get probably negative result */
        fprintf(fpp, "%s\n", res[ct]);  /* Write it */

        fclose(fpp);   /* Close result file */
}
printf("Do you wish to use the Expert System(Y/N)?");
x = toupper(getch());

if (x == 'N') {     /* Don't want to use system */
    printf("\n\nExpert System Data Base is loaded\n");
    exit(0);
}
```

(Fig. D-4 cont.)

```c
    /* Want to use system */

    /* Open data base and result files */
    if ((fp = fopen("xpbase", "r")) == NULL) {
        printf("Data Base Unavailable\n");
        exit(0);
    }

    if ((fpp = fopen("xpresult", "r")) == NULL) {
        printf("Data Base Results Unavailable\n");
        exit(0);
    }

    x = y = ct = 0;

    /* Get information from files and write it back into arrays */
    while (fgets(ques, 200, fp) != NULL) {
        sscanf(ques, "%lf:%lf:", &z[ct][0], &z[ct][1]);
        fgets(q[ct++], 200, fp);
    }

    ct = 0;

    while (fgets(res[ct++], 99, fpp) != NULL)
        ;
        fclose(fp);   /* Close data base file */
        fclose(fpp);  /* Close result file */

        printf("\n\nData base has been loaded into memory\n");

        x = y = ct = 0;

    /* Into expert system */

        printf("EXPERT SYSTEM\n\n");
        printf("    MAMMALS\n\n");

        while (y > -1 && y < 1 && ct < 5) { /* While valid questions */
            printf("%s\n", q[ct]); /* Display question */
            x = toupper(getch());  /* Get keyboard response */
            if (x == 'Y')
                x = 0;  /* Positive answer equates to zero */
            else if (x == 'N')
                x = 1;  /* Negative answer equates to 1 */
            else {      /* Don't know answer */
                ++ct;
                continue;  /* Move on. Don't increment y */
            }

            /* Either a 'Y' or 'N' has been the reaponse */
            y += z[ct++][x]; /* Increment y by value in z[][] */

        }

        /* Determination Rules */
```

(Fig. D-4 cont.)

```c
        if (y >= 1.0)
              puts(res[0]);
        else if (y <= -1.0)
              puts(res[1]);
        else if (y > 0)
              puts(res[2]);
        else if (y < 0)
              puts(res[3]);
        else
              printf("Not enough information to decide\n");
}
```

Fig. D-5. This expert system learns by trial and error.

```c
main()
{
        int i, x, y, qrs[40], t[40];
        char ry[80], rn[80], f[80], e[40][80],num[20];

        printf("How many questions will be used? ");
        gets(num); /* Write number of questions to num */

        y = atoi(num); /* Convert value in num to numeric quantity */

        for (i = 0; i < y; ++i) { /* Loop from 0 to y - 1 */
             qrs[i] = t[i] = 0;/* Initialize qrs[] and t[] to zero */
             printf("Question #%d: ", i); /* Question prompt */
             gets(e[i]); /* Write user question to e[i] */
        }

        printf("\n\nName the first of two results\n");
        gets(ry); /* First result */
        printf("Name the other result\n");
        gets(rn);  /* Alternate result */

        while (ry) {   /* Endless loop */
              for (i = 0 i < y; ++i) {  /* Loop from 0 to y - 1 */
                   qrs[i] = 0;
                   printf("%s(Y/N)? ", e[i]); /* Print question */
                   gets(f); /* 'Y' or 'N' */
                   if (tolower(f[0]) = 'y') /* Make lower case */
                        qrs[i] = 1;   /* if 'y' then 1  else 0 */
              }

              x = 0;
              for (i = 0; i < y; ++i)  /* Display results */
                    printf("%d    %d\n", qrs[i], t[i]);
              for (i = 0; i < y; ++i)  /* Loop again */
                    x += qrs[i] * t[i];  /* Learning sequence */

              if (x >= 0) {
```

(Fig. D-5 cont.)

```
                    /* x is >= 0 */
                    printf("The result is %s\n", ry);/* First result */
                    printf("Is this correct(Y/N)?\n");  /* \correct */
                    gets(f);
                    if (tolower(f[0]) = 'y')
                        continue; /* It's Ok, go around again */
                    else      /* Wrong result */
                        for (i = 0 i < y; ++i)
                            t[i] -= qrs[i];  /* Relearning sequence */
            }

            if (x < 0) {              /* Less than zero */
                printf("The result is %s\n", rn); /* Alternate result */
                printf("Is this correct(Y/N)?\n");  /* \ok? */
                gets(f);
                if (tolower(f[0]) == 'y')
                    continue;     /* OK    go around again */
                else       /* Wrong!! */
                    for (i = 0 i < y; ++i)
                        t[i] += qrs[i];  /* Relearn */
            }
        }
    }
```

Fig. D-6. This modification allows learning to be saved.

```
    main()
    {
        int i, x, y, qrs[40], t[40];
        char ry[80], rn[80], f[80], e[40][80],num[20];
        FILE *fp, *fpp;

        printf("How many questions will be used? ");
        gets(num);  /* Get total number of questions to num[] */

        y = atoi(num); /* Write integer value in num[] to y */

        for (i = 0; i < y; ++i) {  /* Loop from 0 to y - 1 */
            qrs[i] = t[i] = 0; /* Initialize qrs[] and t[] to 0 */
            printf("Question #%d: ", i + 1); /* Question prompt */
            gets(e[i]);  /* Write user's question to e[i] */
        }

        printf("\n\nName the first of two results\n");
        gets(ry);  /* Write result 1 to ry[] */
        printf("Name the other result\n");
        gets(rn);  /* Write result 2 to rn */

        while (ry) {    /* Endless loop */
            for (i = 0; i < y; ++i) {  /* loop from 0 to y - 1 */
                qrs[i] = 0;  /* Initialize qrs[i] to 0 */
                printf("%s(Y/N)? ", e[i]);  /* Ask question */
                gets(f);  /* Get 'y' or 'n' to f[] */
                if (tolower(f[0]) == 'y')   /* Make f[0] lower case */
```

(Fig. D-6 cont.)

```
                    qrs[i] = 1; /* if 'y' qrs[i] == 1 else == 0 */
            }
            x = 0;
            for (i = 0; i < y; ++i) /* Loop as before */
                    printf("%d    %d\n", qrs[i], t[i]);  /* Display results */
            for (i = 0; i < y; ++i)
                    x += qrs[i] * t[i];     /* Learning sequence */

            if (x >= 0) {  First determination rule */
                    printf("The result is %s\n", ry); /* guess ry */
                    printf("Is this correct(Y/N)?\n");  /* Correct? */
                    gets(f);   /* Write response to f[] */
                    if (tolower(f[0]) == 'y') {   /* If 'y' */
                            printf("Do you want to continue(Y/N\n");
                            if (tolower(getch()) == 'y')
                                    continue;  /* Loop again */
                            else
                                    break;    /* End */
                    }
            else     /* x is < 0 */
                    for (i = 0; i < y; ++i)   /* Loop again */
                            t[i] -= qrs[i]; /* Alternate sequence */
            }
            if (x < 0) {    /* x < 0 */
                    printf("The result is %s\n", rn); /* Choose result 2 */
                    printf("Is this correct(Y/N)?\n");/* \correct */
                    gets(f);  /* Write answer to f[] */
                    if (tolower(f[0]) == 'y')    /* Answer is correct */
                            continue;   /* continue with sequence */
                    else           /* Answer incorrect */
                            for (i = 0; i < y; ++i)   /* Loop again */
                                    t[i] += qrs[i]; /* Alternate sequence */
            }

    }
    printf("Do you wish to save this data base(Y/N)?\n"); /* Save? */
    gets(f);  /* Yes? NO? */
    if (tolower(f[0]) == 'y') { /* YES */
            fp = fopen("result", "w"); /* Open result file */
            fprintf(fp, "%s%s\n", ry, rn); /* Write ry[] and rn[] to file */
            fclose(fp); /* Close result file */

            fp = fopen("dbase", "w");    /* Open data base file */
            fpp = fopen("determ", "w"); /* Open determination file */

            for (i = 0; i < y; ++i) {   /* Loop through all values */
                    fputs(e[i], fp);         /* Write e[i] to data base file */
                    fprintf(fpp, "%d %d\n", qrs[i], t[i]); /* Write values */
            }
            fclose(fp);     /* Close data base file */
            fclose(fpp);    /* Close determination rule file */

}
```

Fig. D-7. This program incorporates most expert system basics.

```c
#include <stdio.h>
main()
{
    int i, x, y, z[100][100], zt[100];
    char q[100][100], c[240], res[100][100];
    FILE *fp, *fpp;

    puts("Do you want to construct the data base(Y/N)?");
    x = toupper(getch());   /* Get response into x (upper case) */

    if (x == 'Y') {    /* Construct data base */
        y = 0;
        puts("Type all questions that cover the subject area.");
        while (y < 100) {  /* 100 questions max 0 - 99 */
            printf("Question #%d = ", y + 1);
            gets(q[y]);              /* get question to q[y] */
            if (strcmp(q[y++], "end") == 0) /* Check for "end" input */
                break; /* If user input "end" then terminate loop */
        }

        printf("Press <return> to answer questions\n");
        x = getch();    /* Halt execution until <RETURN> */

        i = x = y = 0;
        while (strcmp(res[x], "end") != 0)   /* Loop until "end" */
            while (y < 100) {  /* 100 results maximum 0 - 99 */
                printf("Name a result and answer the questions for that result \n\n\n");
                printf("Result #%d = ", x + 1);
                gets(res[x]);  /* get result into res[x] */
                if (strcmp(res[x], "end") == 0) /* Check for "end" */
                    break;  /* User input "end", terminate loop */

                printf("\n\n\nAnswer the following questions about <%s>.\n\n\n", res[x]);

                /* Loop until q[i] == "end" */
                for (i = 0; strcmp(q[i], "end") != 0; ++i) {
                    printf("%s (Y/N)?", q[i]); /* Display questions */
                    if (toupper(getch()) == 'Y') /* Get response */
                        z[x][i] = 1;   /* Write 1 to z[x][i] */
                    else                /* Response is negative */
                        z[x][i] = 0;   /* Write 0 to z[x][i] */

                    printf("\n");
                }
                ++x;    /* Increment to next array position */
            }
    fp = fopen("adbase", "w");   /* Open data base file */
    fpp = fopen("adques", "w");  /* Open question file */

    i = 0;
```

(Fig. D-7 cont.)

```c
        /* Loop until q[i - 1] == "end" */
        while (strcmp(q[i - 1], "end") != 0)
            fprintf(fpp, "%s\n", q[i++]);  /* Write questions to file */

        fclose(fpp);  /* Close question file */

        i = x = y = 0;

        /* Loop until res[x - 1] == "end" */
        while (strcmp(res[x - 1], "end") != 0) {
            fprintf(fp, "%s\n", res[x]);  /* Write result */
            if (strcmp(res[x], "end") == 0)
                break;   /* If "end" was written, break! */

            /* Nested loop--loop until q[i] == "end" */
            for (i = 0; strcmp(q[i], "end") != 0; ++i)
                fprintf(fp, "%d", z[x][i]);/*Write 1 pattern element*/

            fprintf(fp, "\n"); /* Pattern written, end line with \n */
            ++x;
        }

        fclose(fp);    /* Close result/pattern file */
        printf("Data Base has been saved.\n");
}
else {      /* Don't wish to build data base */
    i = x = y = 0;
    printf("Do you wish to use the data base(Y/N)\n");
    x = toupper(getch()); /* Get response to x */

    if (x == 'N') {   /* Don't want to use Expert--end */
        printf("Data has been saved...exiting Expert.\n");
        exit(0);   /* Terminate execution */
    }

    if (x == 'Y') {   /* Want to use Expert */
        /* Open data base file */
        if ((fp = fopen("adbase", "r")) == NULL) {
            printf("Cannot open data base\n");
            exit(0);
        }
        /* Open question file */
        if ((fpp = fopen("adques", "r")) == NULL) {
            printf("Cannot access question file\n");
            exit(0);
        }

        for (x = 0; ; ++x) {     /* Endless loop */
            fgets(q[x], 80, fpp);/* Write file question to q[] */
            q[x][strlen(q[x])-1] = '\0'; /* Remove newline (\n) */
            if (strcmp(q[x], "end") == 0) /* Check for "end" */
                break;   /* Exit loop */
        }
        for (x = 0; ; ++x) {     /* Another endless loop */
            fgets(res[x], 80, fp);/* Write result to res[] */
            res[x][strlen(res[x]) - 1] = '\0';/* Remove newline */
```

(Fig. D-7 cont.)

```c
                    if (strcmp(res[x], "end") == 0) /* Check for "end" */
                        break; /* If "end", break out of endless loop */
                    fgets(c, 240, fp); /* Write file pattern to c[] */

                    /* Loop til q[i] == "end" */
                    for (i = 0; strcmp(q[i], "end") != 0; ++i)
            /* Write pattern element in c[i] as a number to z[x][i] */
                        z[x][i] = c[i] - '0';
                    }
                printf("Data base has been loaded into memory.\n");
            }
    }

  /* Use Expert System */

  c[0] = '\0';  /* c == NULL */
  while (strcmp(c, "done") != 0) {    /* Loop until c == "done " */
        printf("\n\n\n\n");
        printf("EXPERT\n\n");

        i = x = y = 0;

  /* Loop until out of questions */
        while (strcmp(q[x], "end") != 0) {
            printf("%s (Y/N)? ", q[x]); /* Print question */
            y = toupper(getch()); /* Get Y/N response */
            if (y == 'Y')   /* Positive response */
                    zt[x++] = 1;   /* 1 == 'Y' */
            else                    /* Negative response */
                    zt[x++] = 0;   /* 0 == 'N' */

            printf("\n");
        }

            /* Loop until res[x] == "end" */
            for (x = 0; strcmp(res[x], "end") != 0; ++x) {
                y = 0;
             /* Nested loop -- loop until q[i] == "end" */
                for (i = 0; strcmp(q[i], "end") != 0; ++i) {
    /* Compare each pattern element in zt with each element in z */
                    if (zt[i] != z[x][i]) { /* If a mismatch is found */
                        y = 40; /* y = 40 means no match found */
                        break; /* Exit nested loop; get new pattern */
                    }
                    else y = 3; /* No mismatch so far */
                }

                if (y == 3) /* Success! A perfect match of all pattern
   elements was found print the result that accompanies pattern */
                    printf("The result is %s\n", res[x]);
            }

            if (y != 3) /* No match. Result not in data base */
                printf("The answer cannot be determined.\n");
```

(Fig. D-7 cont.)

```
                printf("\n\n\nDo you want to quit(Y/N)\n"); /* Quit?? */
                x = toupper(getch());
                if (x == 'Y') /* Yes. Quit! */
                    strcpy(c, "done"); /* c == "done"; while loop exit clause */

        }

    }
```

Fig. D-8. This program can be modified to identify anything.

```
/* Teaching program for animal identification */
#include <stdio.h>
main()
{
    char creature[100][100];
    char quesm[100][100], name[30], code[200], fname[30];
    char *p, *f, question[100], animal[40], c[100], d[10];
    int i, k, q, x, y, z;
    FILE *fp, *fpp;

    for (x = 0; x < 100; ++x) /* Initialize quesm[] and */
        quesm[x][0] = creature[x][0] = '\0'; /* to '\0' */

    for (x = 0; ; ++x) {  /* Endless loop */
        printf("Name an animal that is not a part of the data base: ");
        gets(animal);    /* Get animal name -- one word */
        strupr(animal); /* Make all chars upper case */

        y = 0;
        while (creature[y][0] != '\0') { /* While list not at end */

            /* If animal name already exists */
            if (strncmp(creature[y++], animal, strlen(animal)) == 0) {
                printf("Animal already exists in data base\n");
                y = -1;  /* Go back 1 count */
                break; /* Break out of while loop */
            }
        }

        if (y == -1) {  /* Identical animal */
            --x;        /* Count back to previous loop value */
            continue;   /* FOR loops again */
        }

        strcpy(creature[y], animal);  /* Animal OK, copy to array */

        printf("Type a question that pertains to the %s\n", animal);
```

(Fig. D-8 cont.)

```c
        gets(question);   /* Write question to question[] */
        strupr(question); /* Make question upper case */

    y = 0;

     /* While animal list not at end */
    while (strcmp(creature[y], animal) != 0) {
        /* Display animal name and question */
        printf("\n\n%s:\n%s(Y/N)? ", creature[y], question);
        z = toupper(getch()); /* Does it apply, Y or N */
        if (z == 'Y')   /* Positive answer */
            z = 1;        /* z == 1 */
        else if (z == 'N')  /* Negative answer */
            z = 0;         /* z == 0 */
        else {              /* Illegal answer */
            --y;            /* Go back to former loop value */
            continue;       /* Try it again */
        }

        sprintf(c, "%d", z);  /* Write value in z to c[] */
        strcat(creature[y++], c); /* Concatenate c to creature[] */
    }

    i = y;
    strcpy(quesm[y], question); /* Copy question to array */
    strcat(creature[y], " ");   /* Put a space after animal name */

    /* Loop til end of list */
    for (y = 0; quesm[y][0] != '\0'; ++y) {
        /* Print animal name and question */
        printf("\n\n%s:\n%s(Y/N)", animal, quesm[y]);
        z = toupper(getch()); /* Does this question apply */
        if (z == 'Y')   /* Yes */
            z = 1;        /* z == 1 */
        else if (z == 'N')   /* No */
            z = 0;           /* z == 0 */
        else {               /* Illegal answer */
            --y;             /* Go back to last loop cycle */
            continue;        /* Try it again */
        }
        sprintf(c, "%d", z);    /* Write value in z to c[] */
        strcat(creature[i], c); /* Copy pattern to end of array */
    }
    printf("\n\nContinue(Y/N)?\n"); /* Do another */
    z = toupper(getch());   ?* Get user response from keyboard */
    if (z == 'N') {     /* End program */
        fp = fopen("creature.dat", "a"); /* Open animal file */
        fpp = fopen("quesm", "a"); /* Open question file */
        for (x = 0; creature[x][0] != '\0'; ++x) {
            /* Write data in arrays to files */
            fprintf(fp, "%s\n", creature[x]);
            fprintf(fpp, "%s\n", quesm[x]);
        }
        fclose(fp);    /* Close animal file */
        fclose(fpp);   /* Close question file */
```

(Fig. D-8 cont.)

```
                    break;          /* Break out of program */
            }
        }
    }
```

Fig. D-9. It loads its database from disk.

```c
#include <stdio.h>
main()
{
    char creature[100][100];
    char quesm[100][80], name[30], code[200], fname[30];
    char *p, *f, question[100], animal[40], c[100], d[10];
    int i, k, q, x, y, z, end;
    FILE *fp, *fpp;

    for (x = 0; x < 100; ++x)  /* Initialize arrays to null */
        quesm[x][0] = creature[x][0] = '\0';

    puts("Do you wish to use the Expert System(Y/N)?\n");
    x = toupper(getch()); /* Get user response to x */
    if (x == 'N')  /* Don't want to use system */
        exit(0);   /* End program */
    else {         /* Want to use system */
        /* Open animal name/pattern file */
        if ((fp = fopen("creature.dat", "r")) == NULL) {
            puts("Cannot open data base file");
            exit(0);
        }
        /* Open question file */
        if ((fpp = fopen("quesm", "r")) == NULL) {
            puts("Cannot open data base question file");
            exit(0);
        }

        x = 0;
        /* Load information from file into animal array */
        while ((fgets(creature[x], 100, fp)) != NULL) {
            creature[x][strlen(creature[x]) - 1] = '\0';
            ++x;
        }

        fclose(fp);  /* Close animal file */

        x = 0;
        load data in question file into quesm[] */
        while ((fgets(quesm[x], 100, fpp)) != NULL) {
```

(Fig. D-9 cont.)

```
            quesm[x][strlen(quesm[x]) - 1] = '\0';
            ++x;
        }

        fclose(fpp);    /* Close question file */
}
```

Fig. D-10. It loads and stores its database.

```c
#include <stdio.h>
main()
{
    char item[100][100];
    char quesm[100][80], name[30], code[200], fname[30];
    char *p, *f, question[100], result[40], c[100], d[10];
    int i, k, q, x, y, z, count;
    FILE *fp, *fpp;

    while (k != '1' && k != '2') {  /* Respond with a 1 or a 2 */
        puts("Type 1 to use Expert System -- 2 to add to (build) data bas
        k = toupper(getch());  /* Get keyboard character to k */
    }

    for (x = 0; x < 100; ++x) /* Initialize array elements to null */
        quesm[x][0] = item[x][0] = '\0';

    if (k == '1')  /* Want to use expert */
        goto qrp; /* Branch to label qrp: */

    /* Else, want to build or add to data base */
    /* Open both files if they exist */
    if ((fp = fopen("fibase.dat", "r")) != NULL && (fpp = fopen("quesfile"
"r")) != NULL) {  /* Files don't exist if NULL is returned */
        x = 0;   /* If execution chain reaches here, files exist */
        while ((fgets(item[x], 100, fp)) != NULL) { /*Get file item */
            item[x][strlen(item[x]) - 1] = '\0'; /* Get rid of \n */
            ++x; /* Get next file item */
        }

        x = 0;
        /* Get questions from question file */
        while ((fgets(quesm[x], 100, fpp)) != NULL) {
            quesm[x][strlen(quesm[x]) - 1] = '\0';  /* Scratch \n */
            ++x;  /* Advance to next array position */
        }

        fclose(fp);   /* Close fibase.dat */
        fclose(fpp);  /* Close quesm */
    }
```

(Fig. D-10 cont.)

```c
        count = 0;  /* Assume start of array */
        for (x = 0; ; ++x) {
            if (quesm[x][0] != '\0') {  /* If there's something there */
                ++count;                 /* Increment count */
                continue;                /* Loop again */
            }

            printf("Name an item that is not a part of the data base: ");
            gets(result);   /* Get item name -- one word */
            strupr(result); /* Make item name upper case */

            y = 0; /* Start at top of list */
            while (item[y][0] != '\0') { /* While not at list end */
                   /* Next line checks for duplicates--ignores \" */
                   if (item[y][0] != '\"' && strncmp(item[y], result,
   strlen(result)) == 0) {
                        printf("Item already exists in data base\n");
                        y = -1;  /* Bad item, count back one cycle */
                        break;   /* Break out of loop */
                   }

                   y++;
            }
            if (y == -1)     /* Duplicate item */
                   continue; /* \try it again */

            strcpy(item[y], result); /* \good item -- copy it */

            printf("Type a question that pertains to the %s\n", result);
            gets(question); /* \get user question */
            strupr(question);/* Make it upper case */

            y = 0;
            while (strcmp(item[y], result) != 0) {   /* While valid list */
                   /* Write item and question to monitor */
                   printf("\n\n%s:\n%s(Y/N)? ", item[y], question);
                   z = toupper(getch());  /* True? 'Y' or 'N' */
                   if (z == 'Y')
                        z = 1;   /* Answer is positive */
                   else if (z == 'N')
                        z = 0;           /* Negative answer */
                   else if (z == 'I')   /* Ignore */
                        z = 3;           /* pattern of 3s */
                   else {                /* Illegal response */
                        --y;             /* Count back 1 */
                        continue;        /* Try again */
                   }

                   sprintf(c, "%d", z);    /* Copy pattern element to c[] */
                   strcat(item[y++], c);  /* Concatenate c[] to item[] */
            }

            i = y;
            strcpy(quesm[y], question); /* Copy the question */
            strcat(item[y], " ");       /* Add space separator between pattern */
            for (y = 0; quesm[y][0] != '\0'; ++y) { /* \loop til list ends */
                   printf("\n\n%s:\n%s(Y/N)", result, quesm[y]);
```

200 Appendix D

(Fig. D-10 cont.)

```c
            z = toupper(getch()); /* Get answer */
            /* This section same as before */
            if (z == 'Y')
                z = 1;
            else if (z == 'N')
                z = 0;
            else if (z == 'I')
                z = 3;
             else {
                --y;
                continue;

                }
                sprintf(c, "%d", z);
                strcat(item[i], c);
            }

            printf("\n\nContinue(Y/N)?");   /* Continue? */
            z = toupper(getch());
            puts(" ");
            if (z == 'N') {      /* Want to end */
                /* Open disk files */
                if ((fp = fopen("fibase.dat", "a")) == NULL) {
                    puts("Can't Write fibase.dat");
                    exit(0);
                }
                if ((fpp = fopen("quesfile", "a")) == NULL) {
                    puts("Can't write quesfile");
                    exit(0);
                }
                /* Write information to disk */
                for (x = count; item[x][0] != '\0'; ++x) {
                    fprintf(fp, "%s\n", item[x]);
                    fprintf(fpp, "%s\n", quesm[x]);
                }
                fclose(fp);     /* Close  "fibase.dat" */
                fclose(fpp);    /* Close "quesfile" */

                break;
            }
        }
qrp:
    puts("Do you wish to use the Expert System(Y/N)?\n");
    x = toupper(getch());
    if (x == 'N')
        exit(0);
    else {        /* Want to use system */
        /* Open disk files */
        if ((fp = fopen("fibase.dat", "r")) == NULL) {
            puts("Cannot open data base file");
            exit(0);
        }
        if ((fpp = fopen("quesfile", "r")) == NULL) {
            puts("Cannot open data base question file");
            exit(0);
        }
```

(Fig. D-10 cont.)

```
            x = 0;
            /* Write information from files to ayyary */
            while ((fgets(item[x], 100, fp)) != NULL) {
                item[x][strlen(item[x]) - 1] = '\0';
                ++x;
            }

            fclose(fp);

            x = 0;
            while ((fgets(quesm[x], 100, fpp)) != NULL) {
                quesm[x][strlen(quesm[x]) - 1] = '\0';
                ++x;

            }

            fclose(fpp);

    }
qrd:
    printf("\n\n\n\n\n\n\n\n\n\n\n\n\n\n\n\n");

    printf("                        EXPERT SYSTEM\n\n");

    c[0] = d[0] = name [0] = fname[0] = code[0] = '\0';

    i = q = x = y = 0;
    for (x = 0; quesm[x][0] != '\0'; ++x) { /* Loop til list ends */
        printf("\n\n%s(Y/N)? ", quesm[x]); /* Ask question */
        y = toupper(getch());
        if (y == 'Y')
            y = 1;
        else if (y == 'N')
            y = 0;
        else {
            --x;
            continue;
        }

        sprintf(d, "%d", y); /* Write pattern element to string */
        strcat(c, d);  /* Build pattern in string */

        i = 0;
        for (z = q; item[z][0] != '\0'; ++z) { /* Compare all patterns */
            sscanf(item[z], "%s %s", name, code);
            if (strncmp(c, code, strlen(c)) == 0) {
                ++i;   /* Another pattern may match */
                if (i == 1) {  /* Switch i to 1 */
                    strcpy(fname, name); /* Copy possible result */
                }
                else if (i == 2) { /* No other possible match */
                    i = 0;   /* Switch i to zero */
                    break;   /* Break out of loop */
                }
            }
```

(Fig. D-10 cont.)

```
            }
            if (i == 1) /* We have an answer */
                break;
        }
        /* Display result */
        printf("\n\n\nI believe you have described %s.\n", fname);
        printf("\n\nDo you wish to continue(Y/N)?%c\n", 7);

        x = toupper(getch());
        if (x == 'Y')
            goto qrd;


}
```

Index

A
absolute truth, 33, 34
access, 164
accidents (see anomalies)
additive law of chance, 39-41, 42
anomalies, 45, 56
   mathematical percentages for, 57-60
ANSI standards, Turbo C and, 11
append operations, 149, 164
applications of C language, 7-8
arrays, 52
artificial intelligence
   C language and, 1-9
   data management for, 79-96
   emotions and, 65
   expert systems and, 97
   Guess My Number game as example of basic, 71-77
   logic vs., 77
   programming "instinctive" intelligence in, 40
   programming with, 9
   single emulation of human thought in, 69-77
   "thinking" process evolution of, 68
   true intelligence vs., 34
   Turbo C and, 11
Assembler, 2, 4
   BASIC equivalent functions in, 5-7
   calling routines in, 7
   increasing program speed with, 8
assembly language programs, 2
atof(), 117, 141
atoi(), 123, 141

B
BASIC, 2, 3, 13, 41
   Assembler equivalent functions in, 5-7
   programming difficulties with, 4
   RUN/C Interpreter for users of, 13
   syntax of, 7
batch files, 12
BCPL language, 1
Bell Laboratories, C language development by, 1
best guess program, 106, 186
binomial events, 45
Binomial Formula, 45-48
   C language function for, 48-60
binomial(), 48
   commented program listing for, 167-168
biological expert systems, simple, 102-110
branching, 159
Break Make On option, Project option, Main Menu, 21
break statements, 123, 137, 140, 144
Build All option, Compile option, Main Menu, 21

C
C language
   applications for, 7-8
   artificial intelligence and, 8
   Binomial Formula function in, 48-60
   calling Assembler routines from, 7
   complex math formulas and, 55
   development of, 1
   increasing program speed with Assembler for, 8
   syntax of, 7
   Turbo C and (see Turbo C), 11-31
calling routine, 169
   main(), 51
calloc(), 83-86
case, upper and lower, 107, 113, 124, 130
chance, 33-60
   additive law of, 39-41, 42
   binomial events and, 45
   computers and, 34
   laws of, 35-48
   laws of, anomalies to, 45
   multiplicative law of, 41-48
   proportionate law of, 35-39
   ratios of, 40
Change Dir option, File option, Main Menu, 19
Clear Project option, Project option, Main Menu, 21
Code Generation option, Compiler option, Options option, Main Menu, 22
colon, scanning stop at, 117
commented program listings, 167-203

compact memory model, 27
Compile option, Main Menu, 17, 20
   Build All option, 21
   Compile to OBJ, 20
   Link EXE option, 20
   Make EXE File option, 20
   Primary C File option, 21
Compile to OBJ option, Compile option, Main Menu, 20
Compiler option, Options option, Main Menu, 22
compilers
   Lattice C, 13
   Mark Williams C, 13
   memory models for, 26
   Microsoft C, 13
   performance comparisons among, 25
   speed of, 13
   Turbo C, 11
continue statements, 146, 165
custom features, 3

D

data access
   management of, 79-96
   virtual filekeeping functions for, 80-95
data management, 79-96
databases, 110
   append operations for, 149
   building, 144, 159
   expert systems, 99
   loading, 136, 150-152, 159, 198-203
   loading questions into, 140
   variable, 111, 187-190
Debug option, Main Menu, 17, 23
default settings, Turbo C, 24
Defines option, Compiler option, Options option, Main Menu, 22
dice roll games, 41
Directory option, File option, Main Menu, 19
disk drive requirements, 14-16
documentation, Turbo C, 24
DOS file interface, Turbo C and, 13
double precision floating point numbers, 49, 50, 52
double quotes, multiple results signified by, 164-166
dumps, 127, 164

E

Edit option, Main Menu, 17, 19-20

else, 138, 154
else-if statements, 104, 120
expert plumber example, 99-102
emotions, artificial intelligence vs., 65
emulations, 66
   AI, human thought, 69-77
   computer program for, 69-70
endless loop, 123, 144, 163, 165
Environment option, Options option, Main Menu, 23
Errors option, Compiler option, Options option, Main Menu, 23
exit(), 123
expert guessing, 143-158, 186
expert systems, 97-166
   accessing, 164
   anticipating all questions and answers to, 109-110
   append operations to databases in, 149
   basic program for, 131-133, 193-196
   building of, 101
   "cannot determine" prompt, 120
   databases for, 99
   defining scope of, 98-99
   else-if statements for, 104, 120
   expert guessing in, 143-158
   expert plumber example of, 99-102
   generic, 110-121
   if-else construct for, 109
   learning in, 147
   line program for, 159-166
   loading data into, 117-118, 198-203
   mathematical nature of, 62
   memory requirements for, 79
   modification program for basic, 197-198
   multiple questions, values on data, 105
   negative answers in, 115
   overwriting of memory area in, 149
   pattern recognition in, 129-143
   processing section of (vehicle), 103
   program listings for, 185-202
   prompting, 114
   questioning, 100, 103, 107, 114, 119, 142
   safety feature for, 148
   sample output for, 157
   sampling for, 99
   saving information in, 127-129
   simple biological sample of, 102-110
   simple program illustration of, 70
   speed and efficiency in, 155
   trial and error in, 121-127

values on data in, 105, 107
variable databases in, 111
external variables, 82

F

F1 Help key, 17
fclose(), 115, 135, 136, 149
fgetc(), 80
fgets(), 80, 116, 117, 138-140, 150, 164
File option, Main Menu, 17, 18-19
   Change DIR option in, 19
   Directory option in, 19
   Load option in, 18
   New option, 18
   OS Shell option in, 19
   Pick option in, 18
   Quit option in, 19
   Save option, 18
   Write To option in, 19
file pointers, 134
fiptr(), 82
fopen(), 83, 85, 114
for loop, 134, 140, 146, 147, 150, 155, 163, 165
formulas
   complex, C language and, 55
   transporting, 54
fprintf(), 114, 115, 135, 149
fputf(), 80
fractions, 40
fscanf(), 80, 116
ftell(), 90
functions, customizing, 3

G

Galileo's proportionate law (see chance; proportionate law of chance)
game playing, 61-78
generic expert systems, 110-121
getch(), 80, 107, 113, 116, 130, 134
getmem(), 84
gets(), 80, 114, 115, 123, 124, 134, 144
global arrays, 52, 53, 54, 169
goto statements, 159
graphics cards, 14, 15
Guess My Number game, 71-77, 173-177
guessing
   definition of, 143
   expert, 143-158

H

header file, 179

help, 17
high-level languages, 2, 3
huge memory model, 28

I

if statements, 113, 114, 118, 125, 130, 136, 138, 140, 159, 163, 164
if-else construct, 109, 138, 154
inference,
  expert systems, 91
  statistical, 34
initialization, memory file, 82
integrated development environment, 16
  leaving, 28-29
intelligence
  artificial vs. true, 34
  guessing and, 143
  instinctive vs. artificial, 40
  mathematics and, 62-63
  trial and error in learning, 121-127
interactive users menu, Turbo C, 12, 28
  accessing, 16
interpreter
  operation of, 14
  RUN/C, 13
isolated events (see anomalies)

J

Jump Optimization, 31

L

languages, 70
  Assembler, 2, 4
  BASIC, 2
  BCPL, 1
  C, development of, 1
  high- vs. low-level, 2, 3, 4
  LISP, 8, 9, 40, 41
  list-oriented, 8, 9, 40, 70
  object-oriented, 8, 9, 40, 70
  Prolog, 8, 9, 40
  Turbo C, 11
large memory model, 27
Lattice C, 13, 84
learning
  expert guessing system and, 147
  expert systems and, 121-127
  saving information from, 127-129
  trial and error, 121-127
Link EXE option, Compile option, Main Menu, 20
LINK.EXE, 30
linker, 30

Linker option, Options option, Main Menu, 23
LISP, 8, 9, 40, 41
list-oriented languages, 8, 9, 40, 70
Load option, File option, Main Menu, 18
logic, AI vs., 77
loops, 108, 123, 133, 134, 155
  endless, 123, 144, 163, 165
  exiting, 117
  for, 134, 140, 146, 147, 150, 155, 163, 165
  nested, 134, 136
  saving information with, 127
  while, 114, 116-118, 121, 123, 130, 134, 136, 144, 147, 150, 152
low-level languages, 2, 3, 4
lowercase, 107, 113, 124

M

Main Menu, options of, 17
main(), 54
  calling routine, 51
Make EXE File option, Compile option, Main Menu, 20
Mark Williams C, 13
matching variables, 137
math coprocessor, 15
mathematics
  emulations using, 66
  human vs. artificial intelligence in, 70
  music and, 63-69
  universality of, 62-63
medium memory model, 27
memory management, Turbo C, 13
memory models, compilers, 26-28
memory requirements, 14, 29
  exceeding, 29, 149
  expert systems, 79
menus, 12, 16, 17, 28
microcomputer requirements, 14, 16, 25
Microsoft C, 13
Model option, Compiler option, Options option, Main Menu, 22
monitors, 14, 15
multiple results, 164, 165, 166
multiplicative law of chance, 41-48
music, mathematics and, 63-69

N

nested loop, 134, 136
New option, File option, Main Menu, 18
newguess(), 7

NULL, 83
nulling out, 159

O

object-oriented languages, 8, 9, 40, 70
operating system requirements, 15
optimization, 30-31
Optimization option, Compiler option, Options option, Main Menu, 22
options, 17
Options option, Main Menu, 17, 21-23, 32
  Compiler option, 22
  Environment option, 23
  Linker option, 23
OS Shell option, File option, Main Menu, 19

P

pattern recognition, 129-143
PC/DOS, 15
Pick option, File option, Main Menu, 18
pointers, 52, 82, 134
Poisson's Probability formula, 56-60
poisson(), 58-60, 170-171
portability, 1, 8
premises, statistical inference and, 34
Primary C File option, Compile option, Main Menu, 21
primitives, 3, 4
printf(), 50, 80, 107, 113, 118, 123, 124, 134, 138, 153, 164
probabilities, 45
  anomalies in, 45
  C language in, 48
  Poisson's formula for, 56-60
program listings, 167-203
programming
  Assembler and BASIC equivalent commands in, 5-7
  Assembler for, 4
  BASIC difficulties in, 4
  custom features in, 3, 4
  customizing functions in, 3
  high- vs. low-level language use in, 2-4
  primitives in, 3
  Turbo C for, 11
  Turbo C, writing and running, 16-24
progressive formula, transportation to C programs, 54
Project Name option, Project option, Main Menu, 21
Project option, Main Menu, 17, 21
  Break Make On option, 21

Index 207

Clear Project option, 21
Project Name option, 21
Prolog, 8, 9, 40
prompts, 114
proportionate law of chance, 35-39
pseudo-random events, 34, 176
   proportionate law of chance and, 35-39
puts(), 80, 130

Q

questioning, 103, 107, 114, 119, 142
   answer not known to, 104, 120, 185
   expert systems, 100
   multiple results, double quotes for, 164-166
   negative outcome to, 115
Quit option, File option, Main Menu, 19

R

ramdisk, 79-80
RAM requirements, 14
rand(), 35-39, 72
random number generation, 34, 176
   mathematical emulations using, 67
   pseudo-random events with, 35-39
   seeding, 36
ratios, 40
Register Optimization, 31
relationships, variables and, 67-68
return values, 52
return(), 52
rewind(), 89, 181
routines, calling, 7
rules, 109
Run option, Main Menu, 17, 20
RUN/C Interpreter, 13, 14
running Turbo C program, 16-24

S

sample analysis, 44
sampling, 44
   binomial, 45
   expert systems and, 99
Save option, File option, Main Menu, 18
saving information, 127-129, 191-192
scanf(), 80, 103
scanning, colon and, 117
seeding, 36
small memory model, 26
software, AI and, 8, 9
Source option, Compiler option, Options option, Main Menu, 22
speed
   expert systems, 155

increasing, 8
minimum system requirements to achieve acceptable, 16
Turbo C and, 11, 13, 26
sprintf(), 80, 148
srand(), 35-39, 72
sscanf(), 80, 116, 117, 153
static double array, 105
statistical inference, 34
statistics, 33-60
   anomalies in, 45
strcat(), 148, 153
strcmp(), 85
strcpy(), 86, 137, 146, 154
strings, extracting values from, 141
strlen(), 139, 140, 154
strncmp(), 154
strupr(), 144
syntax
   BASIC, 7
   C language, 7
system requirements, Turbo C, 14-16

T

TC.EXE, 16
TCC command line version, 29-30
TCC.EXE, 29-30
text handling, Turbo C, 13
tiny memory model, 26
tolower(), 124
toupper(), 107, 113, 119, 130, 134
transportation, formula, 54
trial and error learning, 121-127, 190-191
triple deep looping (see nested loop)
True/False statements, 33
truth, 33-60
   absolute, 33, 34
   True/False statements and, 33
Turbo C, 11-31
   artificial intelligence programming and, 11
   characteristics and development of, 11-12
   comparisons with other compilers, 25
   default settings for, 24
   documentation of, 24
   DOS file interface in, 13
   editor, 25
   functions and statements equivalents, 13
   integrated programming environment, 16, 28
   interactive users menu, 12, 16
   leaving integrated environment of, 28

Main Menu and options, 17
master directory for, 16
memory management in, 13
operating system requirements, 15
optimization of, 30-31
RUN/C Interpreter and, 13
speed of programs in, 11, 26
system requirements, 14-16
TCC command line version, 29-30
text handling in, 13
use of, 24-25
writing and running, 16

U

unknown answers, 185
uppercase, 107, 113, 124
UNIX, 84
unlink(), 83, 94-95

V

values, 129, 137
   data variables, 105, 107
   matching, 130
   variables assigned, 135
variable databases, 187-190
   expert systems and, 111
variables, 72, 133
   assigning values to, 135
   declaring, 113
   external, 82
   matching, 137
   values of, 105
vclose(), 81, 85, 92-93, 182
vfil.h file, 81-83, 81
vfiloc, 82, 85, 87, 88, 90
vgetc(), 81, 93, 183
vgets(), 81, 88-89, 181
viloc, 85
virtual filekeeping functions, 80-95
vlink(), 81, 83, 92, 94, 183
vopen(), 81, 83-87, 88, 94179
vputc(), 81, 93, 182
vputs(), 81, 87-88, 93, 180
vsek(), 81, 91-92, 182
vtell(), 90, 181
vwind(), 89-90, 181

W

while loop, 107, 114, 116-118, 121, 123, 130, 134, 136, 144, 147, 150, 152
   saving information from, 127
wild card, 165
windows, 17
Write To option, File option, Main Menu, 19
writing Turbo C program, 16-24